Making Headway
Advanced

Phrasal Verbs and Idioms

Graham Workman

Oxford University Press 1995

Oxford University Press
Walton Street, Oxford OX2 6DP

Oxford New York Toronto Madrid
Delhi Bombay Calcutta Madras Karachi
Kuala Lumpur Singapore Hong Kong Tokyo
Nairobi Dar es Salaam Cape Town
Melbourne Auckland

and associated companies in
Berlin Ibadan

OXFORD and OXFORD ENGLISH are trade marks of
Oxford University Press

ISBN 0 19 435542 X
© Oxford University Press 1995

No unauthorized photocopying

Typeset by Wyvern Typesetting Ltd, Bristol
Printed in Malta by Interprint Limited

Acknowledgements

The author would like to thank all those
teachers and students who have commented
on or worked with the materials, and
especially Imogen Arnold, Alistair Banton,
Margaret Bell, Rodney Blakestone, Pamela
Carter, Benita Cruikshank, John Crutchley,
Carmela Di Clemente, Clare Fletcher, Amanda
Jeffries, Horvath Enikö, Pat Lane, Beth Neher,
Sheila Sullivan, Sarah Workman. Thanks, too,
to Sarah Workman for her help with the
illustrations.

Illustrations by

Ros Asquith
Rachel Busch
Sophie Grillet
Nigel Paige
Alex Tiani
Harry Venning

Location photography by

Haddon Davies Photography

The publishers and author would like to thank
the following for their kind permission to
reproduce photographs:

Jim Lowe/Ace
The Ronald Grant Archive
Robert Harding
Robert Harding/FPG International
Rex Features
Mark Harwood/Tony Stone Worldwide
Dale Durfee/Tony Stone Worldwide

Contents

Foreword

Students of English realize very early on in their learning career that prepositions present a problem. They collocate with nouns, adjectives, past participles, and verbs, without rules or logic. Students simply have to learn that *interested* is followed by *in*, and *good* is followed by *at*, and *go home* has no preposition. Multi-word verbs, or phrasal verbs as they are often referred to, present a very special problem. English can make verb and particle (preposition or adverb) combinations easily and freely. The word *particle* has been used throughout this book, in order to avoid having to make the adverb/preposition distinction (to most students, the word after the verb in a multi-word verb is always a preposition). Multi-word verbs exist throughout the language. They express everyday actions such as *Turn on the light*; they can also have a variety of meanings such as *Things worked out well*, *We worked out the problem*, *She worked out in the gym*, *I've never been able to work him out*, and *The final price works out at £10.*

Given the complexity of the area, the surprise is that learners are very keen to master it. They seem to sense that multi-word verbs are a vital component of English, and spoken English in particular. There is also the feeling that an understanding of common idioms will increase their comprehension, though most students instinctively avoid trying to produce them. The best time to address these areas is at upper-intermediate and advanced levels, when students already have a certain grammatical and lexical foundation.

This books goes a long way to helping students to unravel the complexity of multi-word verbs, preposition and adverb collocations, and idiomatic expressions. Students will find staged guidance in understanding the systems, and are given a variety of exercise practice in recognition and production. *Phrasal Verbs and Idioms* will find its place in self-access centres, for learners to study on their own; and teachers will welcome the texts, listenings, explanations, and exercises, which have clear aims and are highly accessible for thorough classroom exploitation.

John and Liz Soars

Series editors

Introduction

Who this book is for

This book is for students who are studying *Headway Advanced* or any other coursebook at a similar level. It can also be used by students who are preparing for Cambridge CAE or CPE examinations.

How the book is organized

The materials in each unit are organized around themes such as personal relationships, money, describing people, health, reviewing books and films, etc. The units are free-standing and can therefore easily be used to supplement a range of coursebooks. As with *Phrasal Verbs and Idioms Upper-Intermediate*, the book is designed to present multi-word verbs in context and illustrate how they are used.

The book contains over 120 multi-word verbs. They have been selected according to the theme of each unit, as well as level of difficulty and usefulness. Practice exercises are provided for consolidation work. Idiomatic expressions which relate to the theme of the unit are also presented and practised.

How to use the book

To the teacher

1 We recommend you use the Introductory unit before any other units in the book. All the units contain enough material for approximately 90 minutes of classroom work.

2 Units 1–10 follow a pattern:

The **Preparation** section is designed as a *brief* lead-in to the theme of the unit, not lasting more than five minutes.
The **Presentation** is usually a listening or reading text, followed by **Checking Understanding**, an activity where the multi-word verbs introduced are matched with specially written definitions.
The **Drills** provide controlled oral practice of the new multi-word verbs. They can be used after the **Checking Understanding** activity, or later, as revision. The drills can be played on cassette, or the teacher can read them aloud in class.
The **Practice** section provides controlled and semi-controlled practice activities for the multi-word verbs introduced in the unit. There are also exercises designed to encourage students to explore the collocations of

some multi-word verbs. This section includes practice exercises for idiomatic expressions.

How multi-word verbs work provides practice in identifying the different types of multi-word verbs, and looks at the general meaning of some particles when used with certain verbs.

The section **What's the answer?** is designed to check that students have understood the important differences between some of the multi-word verbs. It can be used as a game or revision activity.

The **Jokes** provide some light relief. They are related to the theme of the unit and sometimes illustrate humorous uses of multi-word verbs.

The **Speaking** section is designed to provide freer practice of the new multi-word verbs and idiomatic expressions, and gives students the opportunity to use them to talk about their own experiences and ideas. It is sometimes connected to the writing task which follows. This section can be used in a subsequent lesson after students have had time to revise and absorb the new language in the unit.

The **Writing** section provides further consolidation of the language covered in the unit, and is probably best set as homework.

Unit 11 is an exception to this pattern. It deals exclusively with Proverbs. At the back of the book, the **Tapescript** is a useful reference point for students to consult. The **Answer key** provides answers to all the exercises, useful definitions for the idiomatic expressions, and helpful guidance on collocation.

3   It is important that students are given some activities for revising the multi-word verbs they learn in the book. The **Drills** section can be used, and a simple revision activity is for students in pairs to test each other using the definitions in **Checking understanding**. Some multi-word verbs and idioms can be used in a *Find someone who...* activity as a warmer at the start of a lesson. Pairs of students can devise clues for a multi-word verb crossword which can then be used to test other students. Students can be asked to act out some of the dialogues on tape, and their spoken and written errors with multi-word verbs can be used in a *Grammar Auction* game.

To the student working independently

1   Read and listen to the presentation reading and listening texts, using the cassette and the tapescripts. Then do the exercises which follow.

2   Test yourself by listening and responding to the drills on the cassette. Alternatively, use the tapescript of the drills – you can cover up the answer and see if you produce the right response.

3   Work through the written exercises in the book and check your answers in the Answer key.

4   Find a friend to practise the spoken exercises with, or write out what you would say.

5   Do the free writing activities and then find someone who can correct them.

Introductory unit

What are multi-word verbs?

Multi-word verbs are verbs that combine with one or two particles (a preposition and/or an adverb), for example:

*The letters BBC **stand for** British Broadcasting Corporation.*
(verb + preposition)

*This milk tastes awful. I think it's **gone off**.*
(verb + adverb)

*She couldn't attend the meeting so Helen **stood in for** her.*
(verb + adverb + preposition)

If the addition of the particle(s) changes the meaning of the verb in some way, it is usually called a phrasal verb, because it has an idiomatic meaning – the phrase means something different from its component parts. There are many different types of phrasal verb; in this book, we call all combinations of verb + particle(s) *multi-word verbs*.

Literal or non-literal meaning?

Literal meaning

Look at the following example:
*He **ran up** the hill.*

Here the meaning of the verb and the particle have not changed.
*He **ran up** = He ran + up (in the direction of the top of the hill)*

Non-literal meaning

Sometimes the addition of the particle(s) creates a multi-word verb that has a completely different meaning from its components. It has idiomatic meaning.

*He **ran up** a large telephone bill.*

In this sentence, *to run up* = to increase the amount of money you owe.

1   The first three example sentences on this page all have multi-word verbs with non-literal meaning. What do they mean? Use a dictionary if necessary.

2 Look at the multi-word verbs below. Write L next to them if they have a literal meaning and N if they have a non-literal meaning. If the meaning is non-literal, say what it is. Use a dictionary if necessary.

Example

L̄ *She entered the room, **put down** her bag, and sat on the chair.*
N̄ *The army has **put down** the rebellion after a long struggle.*
(*to put something down* = to defeat or suppress something)

a. ☐ She *turned* the exam paper *over* and read all the questions.
b. ☐ They have *broken off* their engagement.
c. ☐ He was very tired and soon *dropped off* in front of the TV.
d. ☐ While repairing the TV aerial he *fell through* the roof.
e. ☐ She always *stood up for* her brother if anyone criticized him.
f. ☐ He *turned* the idea *over* in his mind all day but couldn't make a decision.
g. ☐ She *broke off* a piece of chocolate and gave it to him.
h. ☐ The plan to build a new road *fell through* due to lack of money.
i. ☐ We all *stood up for* the President when he entered the room.
j. ☐ This plant must be dead. All the leaves have *dropped off*.

– **Doctor, I can't get to sleep at night.**
– **Try lying on the edge of the bed –**
   you'll soon drop off.

Semi-literal meaning
Some multi-word verbs have a semi-literal meaning. The basic meaning of the verb remains the same, but the particle adds an extra meaning.

Look at this example:
*After stopping for fuel in New York, the plane **flew on** to Los Angeles.*

Here, the particle *on* gives the idea of continuing to fly. Look at these further examples where *on* has the same general meaning of *continuing with something*.

*I thought of leaving my job, but my boss persuaded me to **stay on**.*
*We thought the ship would stop and pick us up, but it **sailed on**.*
*The road conditions were dreadful, but we decided to **drive on**.*
*We camped near a village for a few days and then decided to **move on**.*
*The soldiers **fought on** despite heavy casualties.*

The meaning of particles

Some particles have the same general meaning when they form both semi-literal and non-literal multi-word verbs. For example, the particle *out* gives the meaning of *something stopping completely*.

a. *This species of bird **died out** in the 19th century.*
= the species became extinct, it **stopped** existing
b. *The room was so hot and airless she **passed out**.*
= she fainted, she **stopped** being conscious

In a. the verb has semi-literal meaning; the basic meaning of the verb 'die' has not changed. In b. the verb has non-literal meaning: *to pass out*

= to faint, to lose consciousness. However, in both cases the general meaning of the particle *out* remains the same.

Knowing the general meaning of some particles when used with certain groups of verbs can help with learning and remembering them.

The same particle can have *different* general meanings when used with different groups of verbs.

3   Look at the multi-word verbs below. Write S if they have semi-literal meaning, and N if they have non-literal meaning.

a. ☐   He jumped into his car and *drove off*.
b. ☐   The plane *took off* on time.
c. ☐   I tried to stop the thief but he *ran off*.
d. ☐   They got into the boat and *sailed off* into the sunset.
e. ☐   We *set off* for the coast early in the morning.
f. ☐   The thieves *made off* when they saw a policeman.

What is the general meaning of the particle *off* when used with the group of verbs above?

4   What is the general meaning of the particle *off* when used with the group of verbs below?

a. Can you *switch off* all the lights when you leave?
b. Management and unions have decided to *break off* negotiations.
c. I was talking to her on the phone when we were *cut off*.
d. The meeting has been *called off*.
e. I must *ring off*. I think I can smell something burning in the kitchen.
f. I'd better *sign off* now or I'll miss the post.

Multiple meanings

The same multi-word verb can have two or more different meanings.

5 Match the different meanings of *pick up* with the definitions below.

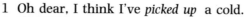

1 Oh dear, I think I've *picked up* a cold.
2 I *picked up* some Chinese while I was in Beijing.
3 He was *picked up* for drink-driving yesterday morning.
4 What time shall I *pick* you *up*?
5 Fortunately the economy is starting to *pick up*.
6 While she was in the bar, two men tried to *pick* her *up*.

a. to improve or recover
b. to collect someone by car or coach
c. to make casual acquaintance with someone, often with a view to having a sexual relationship
d. to learn something without difficulty or special study
e. to catch an illness
f. to arrest someone

Someone and/or *something*
Some multi-word verbs can be used to talk about people **and** things without any difference in meaning.

Example
*I asked her to marry me but she **turned** me **down**.*
*The committee **turned down** my application.*

to turn someone/something down = to refuse or reject someone/something
In this book, this is shown by *someone/something* appearing with the verb.

Some multi-word verbs have a different meaning when they are used about people and when they are used about things.

Example
*We've got a spare room so we can **put** you **up** for the night.*
to put someone up = to give someone a place to sleep

*The landlord has **put** our rent **up** again.*
to put something up = to raise the price or cost of something

When there is a difference in meaning like this, it will be shown with only *someone* **or** *something*, whichever is appropriate.

6 Work in groups. Try to think of as many different meanings as possible for the following multi-word verbs: *to go off* and *to blow up*. Then check your answers with a dictionary or the Answer key.

Collocation

Some words are regularly used together. This is collocation. For example, *to run up* (i.e. to increase the amount of money you owe) collocates with these words: a bill, a debt, an account, an overdraft, and a deficit.

*He's **run up** enormous debts.*
*The company **ran up** a considerable deficit.*
*She's always **running up** an overdraft.*

A good dictionary can help with collocation, since it will give examples of words that are often used with certain verbs. It will show that sales, orders, sterling, the economy, and someone's health, can all *pick up* (= to improve or recover). Similarly, an idea, a plan, a project, an arrangement, a scheme, and a proposal, can *fall through* (= to be abandoned or fail to be completed).

It is important to know which words or phrases collocate with multi-word verbs. For example, *to go off* = to go bad. It is possible to say that milk, eggs, meat and fish have *gone off*. But it is not possible to use this multi-word verb with bread, vegetables or other kinds of food – they do not collocate.

7 Which of the words can be used with the multi-word verbs below? Up to three items can be correct.

1 They have called off
    a. the excursion.
    b. the football match.
    c. the 6.50 train to Oxford.
    d. their subscription to the magazine.

2 What time did
    a. the party   break up?
    b. the film
    c. the journey
    d. the meeting

The style of multi-word verbs

Multi-word verbs are frequently used in everyday spoken and written English, and they usually have an informal style. In more formal contexts, some multi-word verbs can be replaced by Latin-based verbs with a similar meaning.

> Can we *put off* tomorrow's meeting till Monday?

Dear Ms Jones,
I am writing to enquire if it would be possible to *postpone* our meeting from 25 July to 2 August.

There is often no single word which can replace the multi-word verb, and an expression with a similar meaning has to be used.

> Dear John,
> We're coming to Luton next week — can you *put us up* for the night?

Hello, this is Mr Bell of Hall Associates. I'm calling about this year's conference. Will the organizers be making arrangements to *provide accommodation* for our sales representatives?

It is important to be careful with equivalent expressions for multi-word verbs, because there can be differences of style. Multi-word verbs are often less formal.

Multi-word verbs most often have a neutral style, and sometimes there is little difference in the degree of formality between multi-word verbs and their equivalents:

*I've **picked up** a cold. = I've **caught** a cold.*

Word order

Every multi-word verb has a rule for word order, and multi-word verbs which have more than one meaning can have several word order rules. Most multi-word verbs belong to one of four basic types.

The four basic types

Type 1 multi-word verbs: intransitive + inseparable

Type 1 multi-word verbs are intransitive (i.e. they do not take an object). Verb and particle cannot be separated.

*The room was so hot and airless that she **passed out**.*
*He was very tired and soon **dropped off**.*

In this book, Type 1 multi-word verbs are written **without** someone or something to show they are intransitive and inseparable: *to pass out*.

Type 2 multi-word verbs: transitive + separable

Type 2 multi-word verbs are transitive (i.e. they take an object). Verb and particle can be separated.

*She's always **running up** bills.*
*Management and unions have **broken** negotiations **off**.*

If an object pronoun (me/you/him/her/it/us/them) is used, the particle must come **after** the object pronoun.

switch off	the light	
switch	the light	off
switch	it	off

In this book, Type 2 multi-word verbs are written with *someone* and/or *something* **between** the verb and the particle to show they can be separated: *to switch something off.*

Type 3 multi-word verbs: transitive + inseparable

Type 3 multi-word verbs are transitive (i.e. they take an object). Verb and particle cannot be separated.

*Can you **look after** the children while we are away?*
*I've **gone off** Peter since he was so rude to me.*

The object pronoun always comes after the particle.

look after	the children
	them

Type 3 multi-word verbs are written with *someone* and/or *something* **after** the particle to show that they are transitive and inseparable: *to look after someone/something.*

Type 4 multi-word verbs: transitive + 2 inseparable particles

Type 4 multi-word verbs are transitive (i.e. they take an object). Verb and particles cannot be separated.

*Her brother's so rude that I don't know why she always **stands up for** him.*
*Don't let me interrupt you; please **carry on with** your work.*

Type 4 multi-word verbs are written with *someone* and/or *something* **after** the two particles: *to stand up for someone/something.*

8 Look at the following sentences and decide if the multi-word verbs are Type 1, Type 2, Type 3, or Type 4.

a. I can't put up with this rudeness any longer.
b. This meat has gone off.
c. I'll pick you up tomorrow morning.
d. CIA stands for Central Intelligence Agency.
e. I can't find my keys. Can you help me look for them?

f. Our plan to emigrate to Australia has fallen through.
g. He drove off very quickly.
h. Could you stand in for me at the meeting?
i. The union has decided to call off the strike.
j. The two countries have broken off diplomatic relations.

More than one type
A few multi-word verbs can behave like Type 1 *and* Type 4:

*Shall I **carry on with** what I was saying?* (Type 4)
*Yes, please **carry on**.* (Type 1)

A few others behave like Type 1 *and* Type 2:

*Did they **close** the factory **down**?* (Type 2)
*Yes, it **closed down** a month ago.* (Type 1)

When a multi-word verb behaves like this, it will be shown in this book
by the use of brackets.

carry on (with something)   *close (something) down*

9 Put the following multi-word verbs under the headings below. Where a
verb can behave like both types, classify it under both headings.

to hit (someone) back   to stand up for someone
to put someone up   to get on (with something)
to run out (of something)   to drop off
to look for something   to ring (someone) back

Type 1   **Type 2**   **Type 3**   **Type 4**

Dictionaries

Dictionaries contain a lot of information about the meaning, collocation,
word order and style of multi-word verbs. Use a dictionary to help you
answer the questions below.

10 What is the difference between:

a. *to bring someone up* and *to bring something up?*
b. *to look something up* and *to look someone up?*
c. *to give up* and *to give something up?*
d. *to make up* and *to make something up?*
e. *to turn in* and *to turn someone in?*

1 In good hands

Preparation

Work in pairs. Look at the diagram below. Add two connected words to each of the categories.

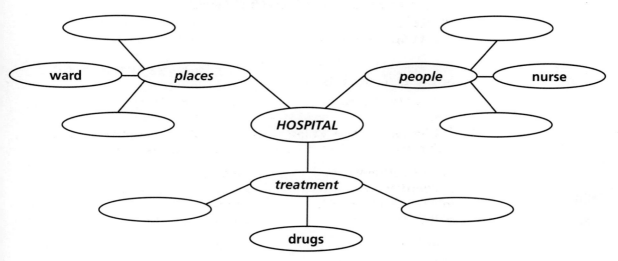

Presentation

T.1a

Listen to a doctor talking to a nurse in a hospital ward. They are discussing four patients. Make notes about the patients in the box below. Then compare your notes with your partner.

1 Mr Harris	
2 Mr Stephens	
3 Mr Spencer	
4 Mr King	

Checking understanding

Match the multi-word verbs in A with the definitions in B. If necessary, listen to the tape again, or look at Tapescript 1a on page 77.

A	B
1 to come through something	a. to feel mentally or physically capable of doing something
2 to build something/someone up	b. to disappear gradually until it no longer exists or has any effect
3 to go ahead (with something)	c. to cause an illness or pain to occur
4 to fight someone/something off	d. to increase the strength, size, or intensity of someone/something
5 to wear off	e. to survive or to recover from a serious illness or situation
6 to bring something on	f. to proceed with something
7 to feel up to (doing) something	g. to overcome or defeat someone/something unpleasant and threatening
8 to try something out (on someone)	h. to test something to see if it is useful or effective

Drills

T.1b

Listen to the sentences on the tape. Use the prompts you hear to make sentences with the same meaning.

Example
Her enthusiasm began to disappear. (*wear off*)
Her enthusiasm began to wear off.

Practice

1 Complete the following sentences, using the multi-word verbs from this unit.

a. My cousin was in a serious car accident last week. Fortunately, he ____ it with only minor injuries.
b. I'm taking lots of vitamin C to help me ____ this cold.
c. We had intended to go out last night, but we were so tired we didn't ____ it, so we stayed at home.
d. Many nervous breakdowns are ____ by stress.
e. The company was finally given permission to ____ with production of the new drug.
f. The dentist told me that when the effect of the anaesthetic ____ , I might feel a little pain.
g. Before you buy a second-hand car, you should always ____ it ____ .
h. I still feel very weak after my illness. I think I need some vitamins to help me ____ my strength ____ .

2 Work in pairs. You and your partner are discussing your neighbours' and friends' illnesses and medical problems. Read through the incomplete dialogue below. Then use the correct tense of the verbs in brackets, and your own ideas, to carry on the conversation.

Example

A Do you ... (*feel up to*) ... dinner?

A *Do you feel up to going out to dinner?*

B No, not really. My teeth still feel funny and ... (*wear off*).

B *No, not really. My teeth still feel funny and the anaesthetic hasn't worn off yet.*

A Hello. How are you today?

B Not brilliant. I ... (*not feel up to*) ... going to work this morning. I've been feeling funny for days, and I'm still trying to ... (*fight off*) ...

A Oh dear. I'm sorry to hear that. Is your sister feeling better?

B Yes, she's over the worst now. The pain ... (*wear off*).

A Oh good. By the way, have you heard about David Smith at number 37?

B Yes, isn't it dreadful? And he's so young, poor thing. Have they decided to operate?

A Yes, ... (*go ahead with*) ...

B What about Jenny next door? How did her operation go?

A Fine. She ... (*come through*) ... , but it'll take her a long time ... (*build up*) ...

B Talking of hospitals, did you see that programme on TV the other day about those doctors who ... (*try out*) ... a new drug and it ... (*bring on*) ... a horrible reaction in the patients?

A Don't tell me! All this talk of illness is making me feel ill.

Collocation

3 Which of the words can be used with the multi-word verbs? Up to three items may be correct.

1 He managed to fight off
   a. his debts.
   b. the enemy.
   c. the pain.
   d. his wound.

2 She didn't feel up to
   a. making a long journey.
   b. working in the garden.
   c. falling in love.
   d. recovering.

3 They decided to go ahead with
   a. the wedding.
   b. their relationship.
   c. the project.
   d. their plan.

4 He came through

    a. a cold.
    b. his injuries.
    c. two world wars.
    d. the crisis.

5 a. The infection   started to wear off.
   b. The wound
   c. The excitement
   d. The pain

Idiomatic expressions

4 Look at the following idiomatic expressions from Tapescript 1a on page 77. What do you think they mean?

a. to be up and about
b. to be over the worst
c. to be in good hands
d. to take a turn for the worse/the better
e. Old habits die hard.
f. to be on the safe side

Think of your own examples for each of them.

How multi-word verbs work

5 *through*

Work with a partner. Look at the multi-word verbs in the sentences below. What do you think they mean?

a. She has had a long and difficult life. She has *lived through* two world wars and a revolution.
b. It was a horrible and painful experience. I never want to *go through* anything like that again.
c. Dr Jones's lectures are long and boring. I refuse to *sit through* any more of them.
d. He's a very heavy sleeper. If a fire alarm started ringing, I'm sure he would *sleep through* it.
e. We both felt much better after we had sat down and *talked through* all our problems.

What is the general meaning of the particle *through* in the examples above?

6 Work in pairs. Discuss the questions below.

   a. What can help people live through a difficult time?

   b. You are in a cinema/theatre, watching a very boring film/play. Do you sit through it or leave? Why?

   c. Why is it a good idea to talk through a problem with somebody else?

What's the answer?

What is the difference between *to come through something* and *to fight something off*?

Jokes

– *Doctor, I've swallowed a roll of film.*
– *Let's hope nothing develops.*

– *Doctor, I think I'm an apple.*
– *Come and sit down. Don't worry, I won't bite you.*

Speaking

Work in pairs. One of you is a patient in hospital, the other is a visitor. Ask your partner how he/she feels, what kind of treatment is being given, and what the doctor has said. Ask questions about the other patients in the hospital ward as well. Use the multi-word verbs and idiomatic expressions from this unit.

Example
Visitor *Hello, how are you today?*
Patient *I feel much better. The doctor says I'll be up and about by the end of the week.*

Writing

Write a short story based on the outline below. Tell the story in the past tense and add a suitable ending. Try to use some of the verbs and expressions from this unit.

> *A young soldier is wounded and captured by the enemy during a war. He is taken to hospital and has an operation. He nearly dies, but eventually he recovers. While he is in hospital, he makes friends with one of the nurses. They fall in love, and she decides to help him escape ...*

2 Floating voters

Preparation

Work in pairs. Discuss the following questions.
– What do you think a 'floating voter' is?
– What are some of the things that influence how people vote at an election?

Presentation

Look at the headlines below. With a partner, try to work out the meaning of the multi-word verbs.

'PM is not up to the job' says Opposition

MINISTER TRIED TO COVER UP ILLEGAL DEALS

GOVERNMENT TO BRING IN NEW ENVIRONMENTAL LAWS

CHANCELLOR FACES UP TO PROBLEMS OF THE ECONOMY

SCANDAL WILL SOON BLOW OVER

GOVERNMENT TO CRACK DOWN ON TAX EVASION

NEW CAMPAIGN TO WIN OVER FLOATING VOTERS

Committee puts forward new energy proposals

MINISTER TO STAND DOWN AFTER CORRUPTION ROW

GOVERNMENT GOES BACK ON ELECTION PROMISES

Checking understanding

Match the multi-word verbs in A with the definitions in B.

A	B
1 to be up to (doing) something	a. to introduce a law, rule or system
2 to cover something up	b. to break a promise or agreement
3 to blow over	c. to be capable of doing something, be of a good enough standard
4 to bring something in	d. to resign from an important position, often in favour of somebody else
5 to face up to something	e. to have the courage to accept and deal with something difficult
6 to crack down on someone/ something	f. to hide something bad, such as a wrong action
7 to win someone over	g. to take strong action against something illegal, or against people who do not obey certain rules or laws
8 to put something forward	h. to cease to arouse interest, to be forgotten
9 to stand down	i. to persuade someone to support or agree with you
10 to go back on something	j. to offer an idea or proposal for consideration

Drills

T.2

Listen to the sentences on the tape. Use the prompts you hear to make sentences with the same meaning.

Example
He isn't good enough to do the job. (*be up to*)
He isn't up to (doing) the job.

Practice

1 Rewrite the following sentences so that they have similar meaning, using the multi-words verbs from this unit.

a. A new law on smoking in public places has been introduced.
b. The government tried to hide its involvement in the gun-running scandal.
c. It is rumoured that the Prime Minister will resign before the next election.
d. Everybody is talking about the seriousness of the problem, but I think it will soon be forgotten.
e. The police are beginning to get tough with young criminals.

f. That's an excellent plan. Are you submitting it to the Committee?
g. The government seems unable to accept or deal with the problems created by its own policies.
h. The new man is well-qualified, but he isn't able to do the job properly.
i. The new government promised not to raise taxes, but it did.
j. Election campaigns are designed to persuade more people to vote for a particular party.

Collocation

2 Which of the words can be used with the multi-word verbs? Up to three items may be correct.

1 The manager tried to cover up
   a. the fortune.
   b. the scandal.
   c. the mistake.
   d. the crime.

2 The police are cracking down on
   a. criticism.
   b. promotion.
   c. traffic offences.
   d. drug smuggling.

3 One should never go back on
   a. one's word
   b. a plan.
   c. an agreement.
   d. a promise.

4 Some people can't face up to
   a. their children.
   b. their responsibilities.
   c. their problems.
   d. the truth.

5 The government is bringing in a new
   a. law.
   b. measure.
   c. policy.
   d. Prime Minister.

6 Who stood down yesterday?
   a. The maths teacher.
   b. The typist.
   c. The Chairman.
   d. The Chancellor.

7 She put forward several
   a. mistakes.
   b. suggestions.
   c. complaints.
   d. proposals.

8 He simply isn't up to
   a. exam standard.
   b. the job.
   c. resignation.
   d. the task.

3 Work with your partner. Discuss the questions below. Use the multi-word verbs you have learnt in this unit.

a. Give two reasons why someone might want to resign from an important position.
b. Think of a scandal that someone has tried to hide from the public.
c. What are some of the ways in which politicians try to win support?
d. What do you think the government or police should be stricter about in your country?
e. What new laws would you like the government to introduce?

Idiomatic expressions

4 Look at the following statements made during an election campaign. What do you think the expressions in italics mean?

a. The government is *out of step* with public opinion.
b. The Minister said he wanted to *keep an open mind* on the issue of subsidizing the public transport system.
c. The government has been *turning a blind eye* to corruption within its own party.
d. People have accused the government of being *out of touch* with what is really going on in the country.
e. The outcome of the election *hangs in the balance*. 'It's very close,' said one commentator. 'No one can say which side will win.'

Which of these expressions has a negative connotation? Which has a positive connotation?

5 Complete the following sentences, using the idiomatic expressions from the exercise above.

a. I don't want to decide until I know all the facts. I want to ____ .
b. He's seriously ill. We don't know if he will live or die. His life ____ .
c. I haven't read any articles on this subject for five years, so I ____ with recent developments.
d. The boss knew his employees were being dishonest, but he did nothing about it. He ____ .
e. Her opinions on this matter are ____ with those of the majority of people.

How multi-word verbs work

Type 1 multi-word verbs are intransitive (i.e. they do not take an object) and inseparable.

Type 2 multi-word verbs are transitive (i.e. they take an object) and separable.

6   Decide if the multi-word verbs in the following sentences are **Type 1** or **Type 2**.

a. The government will bring in new legislation to tackle the problem.
b. He will return to public life when the scandal has blown over.
c. They are putting forward new and radical proposals in their election manifesto.
d. She failed to win over the rebels in her own party.
e. She tried to cover up her involvement in the plan to sell arms illegally.
f. She has decided to stand down as leader of the party.

What's the answer?

1   What is the opposite of *to go back on your word?*
2   What is the opposite of *to be out of touch with something?*
3   What is the difference between the following:
    a. *to bring something in* and *to put something forward?*
    b. *to stand down* and *to resign?*

Joke

Sir Winston Churchill was making a public speech when a woman suddenly shouted out: 'If you were my husband, I'd give you poison.' Churchill replied: 'Madam, if I were your husband, I would take it.'

Speaking

Work in groups of three. You are publicity writers who have been hired to write a pamphlet for the New Environment Party. Discuss the key issues and slogans you want to use in the pamphlet. Think of ways of criticizing the other parties and encouraging people to vote for you.

Writing

Write the text for the pamphlet, using the multi-word verbs and expressions from this unit.

3 Arts review

Preparation

Work in pairs. Look at the list of types of books and films below. Choose two or three categories, and discuss what you like or dislike about them.

SCIENCE FICTION
WESTERN
DOCUMENTARY
THRILLER
ROMANCE
HORROR
CRIME
COMEDY

Presentation

T.3a

Listen to this radio interview. Two people are discussing a book, a play, and a film. Make notes on what they thought was good and bad about each of them. Then compare your notes with your partner.

	Positive	Negative
Book *One Hot Summer*		
Play *The Tempest*		
Film *Suburban Blues*		

Checking understanding

Match the multi-word verbs in A with the definitions in B. If necessary, listen to the interview again or look at Tapescript 3a on page 78.

A	B
1 to bring something out	a. to succeed, to be successful (e.g. an attempt, plan or idea)
2 to make of someone/something	b. to have an impression of someone/something
3 to go on	c. to reach an expected standard
4 to come off	d. to discourage someone from liking someone/something
5 to turn out to be someone/something	e. to communicate or convey something clearly
6 to put someone off someone/something	f. to be understood clearly (e.g. a message or idea)
7 to live up to something	g. to publish or introduce something onto the market
8 to come across	h. to be discovered to be someone/something (eventually)
9 to put something across	i. to happen

Drills

T.3b

Listen to the sentences on the tape. Use the prompts you hear to make sentences with the same meaning.

Example
What did you think of that film on TV last night? (*make of*)
What did you make of that film on TV last night?

Practice

1 Rewrite the sentences below, using multi-word verbs from this unit. Make any necessary changes to the structure of the sentences.

a. Susan Shaw published a slim volume of poetry last year.
b. Our attempt to climb the mountain in winter didn't succeed.
c. Her behaviour was so strange that I didn't know what to think of her.
d. The author conveyed her ideas in very simple language.
e. I couldn't understand what was happening at the beginning of the film.
f. I thought the message of the play wasn't very clear.
g. The newspaper reviews discouraged people from seeing the play.
h. I expected the music to be wonderful, but it wasn't very good.
i. At the end of the film we discover that the hero is an American spy.

2 Work with a partner. Discuss whether the following sentences are correct or not, and why.

a. The film came off.
b. Her attempt to break the world record didn't come off.
c. His message didn't come across very clearly.
d. The book came across very clearly.
e. I made of it a strange film.
f. What do you make of capital punishment?
g. What do you make of this article on capital punishment?

Idiomatic expressions

3 What do you think the following expressions in italics mean?

a. The stage production was absolutely fantastic. It was *out of this world*.
b. He was portrayed as a really gentle person in the film, so I thought it was completely *out of character* for him to shoot his best friend.
c. I had *mixed feelings* about it. I loved the photography, but the acting was dreadful.
d. Don't ask me what the film was about because I couldn't *make head or tail of it*.

How would you express the same ideas in your own language?

His singing is out of this world.

'What do you make of it?'
'I can't make head or tail of it.'

27

Role-play

4 Work in pairs. One of you is a theatre critic, the other is the editor of an arts magazine. Read the notes for your role, and spend some time thinking about what you will say. Then act out the conversation with your partner.

Theatre Critic

You are the theatre critic of *Swinging*, a lively arts magazine. You saw the musical *Heaven and After* and made some notes while watching. Your editor is telephoning you to find out what you thought of the production.

HEAVEN AND AFTER

- I thought it was going to be good, but this is really disappointing
- I didn't understand what was happening a lot of the time
- the scenery wasn't anything special
- the idea of using space-age costumes doesn't work
- I like some things (e.g. the music), but dislike others (e.g. the star singer is awful)
- what _is_ the director trying to say??
- the ending is incomprehensible!

Use the expressions in the box below to help you.

live up to	have mixed feelings	can't make head or tail of it
go on	put across	come off	out of character

Editor

You are the editor of *Swinging*, a lively arts magazine. You are also the parent of the female star of a musical called *Heaven and After*. You want a good review for the production. You are telephoning the theatre critic to persuade him/her to write a good review.

Heaven and After

~ it's had excellent reviews from other critics
~ I thought the musical was going to be very good and it was
~ the sense of mystery and magic was understood very clearly
~ the scenery was fantastic
~ the idea of space-age costumes is really successful
~ the music and singing are fantastic!
~ the director communicates the message of the musical ('only love can save the world') very clearly
~ liked the ending, when we discover it was all a dream
~ please don't discourage people from seeing it!

Use the expressions in the box below to help you.

live up to   come off   put someone off   come across   put across
out of this world   turn out to be

How multi-words verbs work

Some multi-word verbs can be made into nouns by combining the infinitive of the verb stem with the particle.

For example, the verb *to write something up* means to produce a written report on something, usually from notes. Therefore if someone writes a review about a play or a film in a newspaper, it is called a *write-up*. Note that the stress is usually on the first part of the word and it is often hyphenated ('*write-up*).

5   Complete the sentences below with nouns formed from the multi-word verbs in italics.

   a.   He *wrote up* an excellent review of the film in The Times.
      The film had an excellent ____ in The Times.
   b.   All the tickets for the show are *sold out*.
      The show is a ____ .
   c.   The play is about the way in which their marriage gradually *breaks up*.
      The play is about the gradual ____ of their marriage.
   d.   The film is about three men who *break out* of prison.
      The film is about a prison ____ .
   e.   She used to be a famous singer, and now she wants to *come back* and be famous again.
      She is trying to make a ____ .

What's the answer?

What is the difference between:

   a.   *to put something across* and *to come across?*
   b.   *to put something off* and *to put someone off doing something?*

Joke

A young composer had written two pieces of music and he asked the great Rossini to listen to both of them and say which one he preferred. The young man began to play the first piece, but after a short time Rossini interrupted. 'You need not play any more,' he said, 'I prefer the other one.'

Speaking

Think of a film, play or book you have seen or read recently. Tell your partner what it was about, and what you thought of it.

Writing

Write a review for *Swinging* magazine of a book, a play or a film. Say what it was about, what ideas the writer or director was trying to put across, and what you thought of it, using multi-word verbs and expressions from this unit.

4 Going by appearances

Preparation

Work in pairs. Discuss the following questions.
- When you meet someone for the first time, what do you notice most: their clothes? voice? facial expression?
- What do these things tell you about the person?

Presentation

Work in pairs. One of you read text A, and the other read text B. Find out what happened, and why. Then exchange information.

A

Last week, Mrs Alice Woolf, aged 65, was tricked into *handing over* all her savings to a smooth-talking doorstep salesman who said he was selling burglar alarm systems. 'I was completely *taken in*,' she said. 'I know it was foolish to let him *talk me into* giving him all my savings, but he seemed such a nice man. He *came across* as completely honest. But I won't make the same mistake again. Once bitten, twice shy.'

When asked if she thought the man would be caught, she replied, 'I don't think he'll *get away with* it. I'm sure the police will catch him sooner or later.'

B

The police are looking for a well-dressed young man who has been *passing himself off* as a doorstep salesman. Last week, he tricked an elderly lady into giving him all her money as a deposit for a burglar alarm system.

A police spokesman said, 'Unfortunately, it's quite easy for dishonest people to make a living doing this kind of thing. I suppose we all tend to *go by* appearances, and very often it's not easy to *see through* a clean-shaven, well-spoken young man in a good suit, and with a pleasant manner. Appearances can be deceptive, and not everyone is a good judge of character. My advice to people is not to *hand over* any money until they have checked people's references and made sure they belong to a reputable organization. Meanwhile we'll do our best to catch the man who took Mrs Woolf's savings.'

Checking understanding

Work with a partner. Try to work out the meaning of the multi-word verbs in italics in the texts. Then match the verbs in A with the definitions in B.

A	B
1 to hand something over	a. to persuade someone to do something
2 to take someone in	b. to deceive or trick someone
3 to talk someone into doing something	c. to pretend that someone/something is someone/something else
4 to come across as something	d. to give something to someone so that they control or own it
5 to get away with something	e. to give the impression of having a particular characteristic
6 to pass someone/something off as someone/something	f. to judge according to something
7 to go by something	g. to see the true nature of someone/something despite a deceptively pleasant appearance
8 to see through someone/something	h. to escape being punished or criticized for something

Drills

T.4

Listen to the sentences on the tape. Use the prompts you hear to make sentences with the same meaning.

Example
You shouldn't base your judgements on the way people dress. (*go by*)
You shouldn't go by the way people dress.

Practice

1 Complete the sentences, using multi-word verbs from this unit.

a. My sister is a very good judge of character. She can ____ people immediately if they try to deceive or trick her.
b. He escaped from the country by ____ as a tourist.
c. I lent him some money because he seemed an honest person, but after that I never saw him again. I soon realized I ____ .
d. Don't ____ his appearance. He may look nice but he's completely untrustworthy.

   e. When I first met him he ____ as a very indecisive person who didn't
       know his own mind.
   f. The salesman ____ buying a new washing-machine, although my old
       one was fine.
   g. The robber told him to ____ the keys to the safe.
   h. The robbers laughed when the bank manager said: 'You won't ____
       this. The police will catch you one day.'

2 One of the sentences below is correct. All the others have one mistake in
    them. Change the sentences so that they are all correct.

   a. No, you can't have the money. I refuse to hand over.
   b. She came across to be a very decisive person.
   c. They got away several serious crimes.
   d. He passed off himself as a policeman.
   e. You should have seen him through immediately.
   f. I was never taken in by his lies.
   g. He talked me into sign the cheque.
   h. I never go with first impressions.

3 Work in pairs. Take turns asking and answering the questions below. Use
    the multi-word verbs in brackets.

   1 Do you ever base your judgement of people on first impressions?
     Why?/Why not? *(go by)*
   2 What impression do you think you give of yourself when you meet
     someone for the first time? *(come across as)*
   3 What do you think is the best way to avoid being tricked or deceived
     by people? *(take someone in)*
   4 Has someone ever persuaded you to do something that you regretted
     later? If so, what was it? *(talk someone into)*
   5 Imagine you could pretend to be someone else for a whole day. Who
     would you choose to be? Why? *(pass yourself off as)*

Idiomatic expressions

4 Work with a partner. Discuss the meaning of the following expressions.

   a. Once bitten, twice shy.
   b. Appearances can be deceptive.
   c. Honesty is the best policy.

How would you express the same ideas in your own language?
Do you agree that *Honesty is the best policy*? Why?

How multi-word verbs work

5 *into*

The particle *into* can be used with some verbs to give the idea of persuading or forcing someone to do something.

The multi-word verbs below have the following form: verb + someone + into. Using the verbs in brackets, rewrite the following sentences so that they have similar meaning. Make any necessary changes to the structure of the sentences.

Example
His boss made him resign.
(force into)
His boss forced him into resigning.

1 She persuaded me to buy a new coat. *(talk into)*
2 The robbers made the bank manager think they were genuine customers. *(trick into)*
3 The Mafia frightened him so much that he remained silent. *(frighten into)*
4 She had to sell her house in order to pay off her debts. *(force into)*
5 The government was made to feel so ashamed that it took action. *(shame into)*

Now think of your own example sentences for these multi-word verbs.

What's the answer?

What is the opposite of *to talk someone into doing something*?

Joke

> – *How did you know he was a ghost?*
> – *I saw through him immediately.*

Speaking and Writing

Work in pairs. Plan and write a leaflet giving people advice on how to deal with doorstep salesmen. Warn them of the dangers and give at least five 'Golden Rules' to follow. Remember to use the multi-word verbs and expressions you have learnt in this unit.

Writing

Use the multi-word verbs and expressions you have learnt in this unit to write a story which ends with the following words:

It was only then he realized that he had been completely taken in.

5 Money! Money! Money!

Preparation

Work in pairs. Briefly discuss one or more of the statements below, saying why you agree or disagree with it.

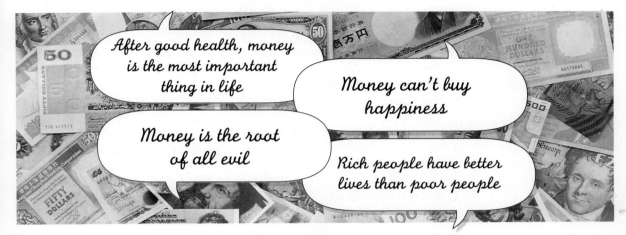

After good health, money is the most important thing in life

Money can't buy happiness

Money is the root of all evil

Rich people have better lives than poor people

Presentation

T.5a

You are going to hear five people talking about money. First, discuss with your partner what you think they will say. Next, listen and make notes. Then compare your notes with your partner.

1 Self-made woman	
2 Rich woman	
3 Bankrupt businessman	
4 Unemployed person	
5 Middle-aged regular saver	

Checking understanding

Match the multi-word verbs in A with the definitions in B. If necessary, listen to the interview again, or look at Tapescript 5a on page 79.

A	B
1 to set out to do something	a. to save something so you can use it later
2 to put something down to something	b. to depend on someone/ something as a source of income
3 to come into something	c. to manage to survive (on something) despite difficulties
4 to live off someone/something	d. to inherit something (especially money)
5 to pay something off	e. to consider something to be the result of something else
6 to keep up with someone/ something	f. to begin with the intention of achieving something
7 to fall back on someone/something	g. to return to someone/something for support, when other things have failed
8 to get by (on something)	h. to progress or rise at the same rate as someone/something else
9 to put something by	i. to repay a debt

Drills

T.5b

Listen to the sentences on the tape. Use the prompts you hear to make sentences with the same meaning.

Example
He intended to win a gold medal. *(set out to)*
He set out to win a gold medal.

Practice

1 Rewrite the following sentences so that they have similar meaning, using the multi-word verbs from this unit. Make any changes necessary to the structure of the sentences.

a. Many pensioners have to survive on very little money.
b. He calculated it would take him three years to clear all his debts.
c. She accumulated a great deal of money by saving a little every week.
d. His uncle died and left him a fortune.
e. She decided she wanted to start her own business.

    f. If I ever get into financial difficulties, I know I can always rely on my brother for help.

    g. She supports herself with the money she gets from selling her books.

    h. She thought she was a success because she had been lucky.

    i. The cost of living is going up all the time, but my salary isn't.

2 Work in pairs. Complete the sentences below without letting your partner see what you have written. Then take turns trying to guess what the other person has written.

    a. If I came into a lot of money, I'd...

    b. One thing I have set out to do, and have achieved, is...

    c. If I earned a salary which didn't keep up with inflation, I'd...

    d. I could get by on very little money provided that...

    e. I put the increase in crime down to...

Idiomatic expressions

3 Look at Tapescript 5a on page 79 and find the idiomatic expressions which mean the following:

    a. to have hardly enough money or food to live on

    b. money is not easily obtained (a saying)

    c. to become less rich and have a lower social status

    d. to live reasonably well without getting into debt

    e. to spend money freely as if it were in endless supply

    f. a time when you might need money

How would you express b. and e. in your own language?

Role-play

4 Work in pairs. Choose one of the situations below. One of you play the role of interviewer. Then change situations and roles. Use the multi-word verbs and expressions from the box.

live from hand to mouth	get by on something
be in the red	put something down to something
come into something	fall back on something
pay something off	set out to do something
live off something	money doesn't grow on trees

Situation 1

You used to have a very poorly paid job, but then you inherited a great deal of money. Describe how your life has changed and what you have decided to do with the money.

Situation 2

You are a self-made man/woman. Describe your poor background, your decision to become rich, your attitude towards money, and how you explain your success.

How multi-word verbs work

Type 4 multi-word verbs are always transitive (i.e. they take an object) and have two particles which are inseparable.

5 The following sentences contain Type 4 multi-word verbs from units 1–5. Fill in the missing second particle.

1 The company has decided to go ahead ____ the new building project.
2 I don't feel up ____ seeing anyone tonight.
3 The police are going to crack down ____ illegal gambling.
4 We must face up ____ our responsibilities.
5 She went back ____ her word not to tell anybody.
6 The speech didn't live up ____ our expectations.
7 During the interview she came across ____ efficient and decisive.
8 They got away ____ using bad language.
9 Inflation is rising so fast we cannot keep up ____ the cost of living.
10 He fell back ____ his savings when he lost his job.

What's the answer?

What is the opposite of :
a. to be in the red?
b. to come/go down in the world?

Joke

> – *My uncle is so mean with money that he refuses to let his children go to school.*
> – *Why?*
> – *Because they have to pay attention!*

Speaking and Writing Look at the picture story below with your partner. Practise telling it with the multi-word verbs and expressions from the box. Then write the story.

live from hand to mouth	put something by for a rainy day
make ends meet	live off something
set out to do something	be in the red
put his success down to	come down in the world
be well off	fall back on someone/something
go up in the world	pay something off
spend money like water	to get by on something

6 Crime doesn't pay

Preparation

Work in pairs. Read the comment below and then discuss how far you agree or disagree with it. Explain why.

'Crime doesn't pay because you always get caught in the end.'

Presentation

Read the newspaper articles below and discuss them with your partner. Then try to work out the meaning of the multi-word verbs in italics.

THE STRAIGHT AND NARROW

The literary world was *taken aback* yesterday when the famous author, Arnold Swift, was found guilty of stealing copies of his latest novel from a bookshop. The magistrate said that he would *let him off* lightly with a £50 fine, but warned him that any further offences would result in a more serious punishment. The novel is called *Keeping to the straight and narrow.*

BREAKDOWN IN LAW AND ORDER

A police spokesman said yesterday that law and order is *breaking down* in some inner-city areas. He was speaking after a night in which two riots had *broken out* and several serious crimes had been reported. 'At present, too many people think they can commit a crime and get away with it,' he said.

HARDENED CRIMINALS

Two men who escaped from prison by hiding inside a cement mixer were recaptured last night when they *gave themselves up* to the police. It seems that the two men, who were described as hardened criminals, had been unable to get very far because of the quick-drying cement that had stuck to their feet. The prison authorities have said they will *set up* a committee to look into security at the prison.

CAUGHT RED-HANDED

Yesterday, Gregory Brush, 24, was convicted of the attempted robbery of a paint factory in Leeds. It was reported that he fell into a large drum of red paint while trying to escape with the money. He was rescued by a nightwatchman and *gave himself up* when police arrived to arrest him. He *owned up* to the crime and pleaded guilty at his trial.

BOMB BLAST

A bomb *went off* in a central car park in the early hours of yesterday morning. Police *sealed off* several streets and *carried out* a detailed search of the area. It appears the bomb was intended for a busy shopping centre nearby.

Checking understanding

Match the multi-word verbs in A with the definitions in B.

A	B
1 to give oneself up (to someone)	a. to prevent people getting in or out of an area or building by closing all the entrances
2 to own up (to doing something)	b. to surprise or shock someone with something contrary to expectation
3 to take someone aback	c. to explode, detonate, or ignite, to make a sudden loud noise
4 to let someone off (with something)	d. to begin suddenly, usually in an unpleasant and violent way
5 to set something up	e. to admit or confess to a crime or to doing something wrong
6 to carry something out	f. to fail, cease or collapse because of a problem or disagreement
7 to go off	g. to establish something, to make the arrangements and preparation for something to start
8 to seal something off	h. to punish someone lightly or not at all (informal)
9 to break down	i. to allow oneself to be arrested or captured
10 to break out	j. to perform or conduct something

Drills

T.6

Listen to the sentences on the tape. Use the prompts you hear to make sentences with the same meaning.

Example
We were shocked and surprised by his rude reply. *(take aback)*
We were taken aback by his rude reply.

Practice

1 Read the newspaper extracts below. Substitute, where appropriate, the multi-word verbs from this unit.

1.

A recent survey, conducted by a national newspaper, shows that the traditional two-parent family is collapsing and is gradually being replaced by single-parent families.

2.

Bank robbers who managed to hide themselves in a time-lock safe in an attempt to steal £3 million, found they were unable to escape when their explosives failed to detonate. They did not resist arrest when security guards opened the safe two days later.

3.

A woman whose 6-year-old daughter was killed by a drunk driver has complained that the judge only gave the man a six-month suspended sentence and a £250 fine. The Home Secretary has said he will be establishing a committee to look into the sentencing guidelines for such cases.

4.

Shortly after the match, fighting suddenly began among the supporters of two rival football teams. The police stopped people entering or leaving the town centre in an attempt to contain the violence.

5.

Jayne Wilson confessed to stealing £15,000 from the company where she worked, when she was caught red-handed by a security camera which recorded her placing the money in her briefcase. 'I was shocked and surprised when I saw the recording,' said the managing director. 'I thought she was someone we could trust completely.'

Collocation

2 Which of the words can be used with the multi-word verbs? Up to three items may be correct.

1 The judge let him off with   a. a warning.
                                      b. a suspended sentence.
                                      c. the death penalty.
                                      d. a two-year prison sentence.

2 They have set up   a. a business.
                                      b. a birthday party.
                                      c. an inquiry.
                                      d. a research team.

3 They have carried out   a. an experiment.
                            b. a committee.
                            c. an inquiry.
                            d. a test.

4 a. The alarm clock   went off.
  b. The fireworks
  c. The gun
  d. The telephone

5 a. A new film   has broken out.
  b. A flu epidemic
  c. A fire
  d. An argument

6 a. Peace talks   have broken down.
  b. The holidays
  c. Negotiations
  d. Community relations

3 Work with a partner. Discuss the following questions, using the multi-word verbs from the box below.

let off	give oneself up	own up to	break down	break out
go off	take aback			

1 What time does your alarm clock start ringing in the morning?
2 Your friend has been involved in a petty crime. It is probable the police will catch him. What would you advise him to do?
3 If you discovered something surprising or shocking about someone you have known for a long time, what would your reaction be ? Give an example.
4 What can cause riots to start suddenly?
5 Which of the following people would you punish lightly or not at all?
  a. a poor woman caught stealing food from a supermarket
  b. someone caught stealing small items from work
  c. a student travelling on a bus without a ticket
  d. a 13-year-old boy caught breaking into a parked car
6 Can you think of examples of people who have been punished lightly for crimes they committed? If so, what were they?

Idiomatic expressions

4 Work with a partner. Look at the expressions in italics and discuss what they mean. How would you express the same idea in your own language?

a. I *caught him red-handed*. When I entered the room I saw him taking the money from my purse.
b. He had *kept to the straight and narrow* all his life, so we were taken aback when we heard he had committed a serious crime.
c. It was a case of *poetic justice*. While the burglar was away on holiday someone broke into his house and stole everything.
d. The judge's responsibility is to ensure that a suitable punishment is given. In other words, *the punishment should fit the crime*.
e. When the man was found not guilty of killing the children, the local people *took the law into their own hands*. They set fire to his house and forced him to leave the area.

5 Work in small groups. Discuss the questions below.

1 A man tries to steal some money from your bag. You catch him red-handed. What do you do?
2 How important is it that people in public life, such as politicians, keep to the straight and narrow in their private lives?
3 What is your reaction when you hear about a case of poetic justice?
4 Why is it so important that the punishment should fit the crime? What is the result if it doesn't?
5 When, if ever, is it right to take the law into your own hands?

How multi-word verbs work

6 *off*

What is the general meaning of the particle *off* when used with the verbs below?

a. They *let off* some fireworks to celebrate.
b. Price increases *sparked off* violent protests.
c. The bomb *went off* without warning.
d. The assassination *triggered off* a civil war.
e. The bomb was *set off* by remote control from a safe distance.

What's the answer?

What is the difference between *to set up* an investigation, and *to carry out* an investigation?

Joke

A set of traffic lights has been stolen from a road junction in Hampstead. A police spokesman said, 'Some thieves will stop at nothing.'

Speaking

A woman is to appear in court charged with murdering a man who had killed her husband and baby daughter in a drink-driving accident. The man had been allowed to go free, with a five-year driving ban and a fine of £250. The woman, shocked by the light punishment, went to the man's house and, after an argument, shot him dead. She then went to the police and admitted killing him.

Work in pairs. Try to think of as many reasons as possible why the woman should be found guilty or not guilty of murder. Decide what you think the result of the trial should be. Then discuss your ideas with the rest of the group.

Writing

A riot was caused by a controversial judgement, in which an apparently guilty man was allowed to go free. Write a newspaper article with the following headline:

COURT CASE SPARKS OFF CITY RIOT

Cover the following points in the article, and use the multi-word verbs and expressions from the box below.

- the result of the court case
- why people were angry
- the shocked reaction of the authorities
- the sudden start of the riot
- how police tried to contain the riot
- the collapse of law and order
- cases of violence and looting
- the sounds of guns firing
- the need for an investigation into the riot

let off   break down   carry out   break out   take aback   go off
seal off   set up
the punishment should fit the crime   to take the law into one's own
hands   to catch someone red-handed

Selling like hot cakes

Preparation

Work in pairs. Using the list below, discuss which things most influence you when you buy something. Then put them in order of importance.

the price	the packaging	the brand name
the quality	the advertising	if it is fashionable

Presentation

T.7a

Listen to a reporter talking to the director of the company that makes *Bubble Up* and *Fizzy Cola*. Then discuss with your partner if the statements below are true or false, and why.

1 *Bubble Up* was an immediate success.
2 The plans for advertising *Fizzy Cola* have changed.
3 The company is doing better this year than last year.
4 The company may go bankrupt.
5 The company will definitely do better in the future.

Checking understanding

Match the multi-word verbs in A with the definitions in B. If necessary, listen to the interview again, or look at Tapescript 7a on page 81.

A	B
1 to catch on	a. to withdraw from an agreement or arrangement
2 to pick up	b. to gain control or possession of something
3 to fall through	c. to be abandoned or fail to be completed (e.g. a plan or arrangement)
4 to come up with something	d. to increase, improve or recover (e.g. economy or business)
5 to take someone on	e. to decrease in amount or number
6 to fall off	f. to employ someone
7 to lay someone off	g. to become popular or fashionable
8 to back out (of something)	h. to produce an idea, suggestion or solution
9 to take (something) over	i. to dismiss someone because there is no work (usually temporarily)

Drills

T.7b

Listen to the sentences on the tape. Use the prompts you hear to make sentences with the same meaning.

Example
This new hairstyle has become popular. *(catch on)*
This new hairstyle has caught on.

Practice

1 Read the dialogue and replace the words in italics with multi-word verbs.

A Hello, Bill, how's the car business doing at the moment?
B Not very well, I'm afraid. Our sales *are decreasing* at the moment, and our latest model hasn't *proved to be very popular*. We've also had to *withdraw from* a new project to build a family car. What about you?
A Our export figures weren't very good at the start of the year, but now they're starting to *improve* and we need to *employ* extra staff. In fact, we're thinking of *taking control of* another business.
B Lucky you! Our company is thinking of *dismissing* some of its staff until things get better. By the way, what happened about that design problem you were telling me about?
A Fortunately one of our team managed to *produce* a brilliant solution to the problem – otherwise the whole project would have *been abandoned*.

Collocation

2 Which of the words can be used with the multi-word verbs below? Up to three items may be correct.

1 She came up with

    a. an interesting idea.
    b. a serious complaint.
    c. a useful suggestion.
    d. the right answer.

2 a. The new fashion   is catching on.
    b. The Prime Minister
    c. The idea
    d. The song

3 a. The plan   has fallen through.
    b. The search
    c. The scheme
    d. The project

4 a. The rain   is falling off.
    b. His love
    c. Investment
    d. Production

3 Write suitable endings for the following sentences.
a. They decided to back out of buying the house when they found out...
b. She took over the company because...
c. The plan to build a new tunnel fell through because...
d. The new fashion didn't catch on because...
e. Sales started to pick up after...
f. Two hundred workers were laid off because...
g. The number of people who want to become nurses is falling off because...
h. Scientists have come up with an idea for...
i. The company took me on when I told them...

4 Look at Tapescript 7a on page 81 and work out the meaning of the nouns below. Then use them to complete the newspaper headlines.

turnover   downturn   takeover   upturn

ECONOMIC NEWS IN BRIEF

*a.*_____ IN ECONOMY WILL INCREASE UNEMPLOYMENT

b. SWEET MANUFACTURER MAKES_____ BID FOR RIVAL COMPANY

c. COMPANY'S ANNUAL_____ RISES BY £30M

d. OPTIMISTIC CHANCELLOR PREDICTS_____ IN ECONOMY

Idiomatic expressions

5 Look at Tapescript 7a on page 81. Find the expressions which mean the following:

a. to begin something badly
b. to sell quickly to many eager customers
c. to start from zero or with nothing
d. to be ruined financially
e. to keep out of debt or difficulty

Using the expressions you found above, what would you say in the following situations?

1 There is an economic recession and you think that a lot of companies will go out of business.
2 You are a supporter of a football club. At the beginning of the football season the team lost all their matches.
3 An engineer designs a new type of engine but then finds it doesn't work. He decides to start again with a completely different design.
4 The company you work for is only just managing to avoid financial difficulties.
5 Your friend has written a novel and it has become very popular. Everyone is buying it.

Now think of further examples using some of these expressions. For example, can you think of something that is selling extremely well at the moment? Can you think of something that started very badly?

Role-play

6 Work in pairs. One of you is the Director of a fashion company, the other is a fashion designer. Read the notes for your role below, and spend some time thinking about what you will say, and the multi-word verbs and expressions you could use in the role-play. Then act out the conversation with your partner.

> **Director of fashion company**
> Your company is not doing well at the moment and you are worried it may go bankrupt. Tell your fashion designer about the latest sales figures, the economic recession, the failure of recent projects, and the need to reduce the number of staff. Find out if he/she has any ideas for helping to save the company.
>
> **Fashion designer**
> You work for a fashion company. The Director has asked to see you about the bad financial position of the company. Try to think of positive things to say about the company, the economy, and your new ideas. Try to think of solutions to the problems the company is facing.

How multi-word verbs work

7 *out*

The particle *out* can be used with some verbs to give the idea of something stopping completely. Look at the sentences below and say what it is that has stopped.

Example
The company backed out of the project.
= The company's participation in the project stopped.

a. The engine was working all right but then it suddenly *cut out*.
b. After two years at university he decided to *drop out*.
c. She had to *pull out* of the competition because of a leg injury.
d. The shop has *sold out* of that style of jumper.
e. This species of bird *died out* in the nineteenth century.
f. They used to be good friends but they *fell out* last summer.

What's the answer?

What's the opposite of the following:

1 sales are *falling off*
2 to get off to a *bad* start
3 a *downturn* in the economy
4 *to lay someone off*

Jokes

FOR SALE: *piano for beginner with legs.*

RESTAURANT
open till closing time

Why ruin your clothes when our modern
WASHING MACHINES
can do the job more effectively?

GRAND PIANO *for sale by a lady in very good condition.*

Speaking and Writing

1 Look at the picture story with your partner. Practise telling the story before you write it. You can decide what happens in picture 12. How do you think the story ends?

2 Now write the story. Remember to use the multi-word verbs and expressions you have learnt in this unit.

8 Crisis? What crisis?

Preparation

Work in pairs. Discuss the following questions.

– In the British parliamentary system, what are the following?
  MP, PM, the Opposition, the Cabinet
– Think of a current political crisis and describe it briefly to your partner.

Presentation

Work in pairs. Read the text and find as many reasons as possible why
the statements below are false.

1 The Government's policy has met with only a little opposition.
2 The Government is prepared to show flexibility.
3 The Government will lose the vote on Wednesday.
4 There is no crisis.

MPs UP IN ARMS AS PM TRIES TO PLAY DOWN CRISIS

There was a strong public outcry yesterday when the Government announced its intention to cut public expenditure on health and education. Opposition MPs were up in arms when the statement was read out in the Commons and immedia.'' *called for* an emergeh. 'e on We 'nesday. Nigel Smith, a n ...r of the Opposition, w ...ticularly outspoken in h .icis" of the Government.

The time has come for ·il of us to *stand up for* what we believe in. Our party *stands for* better health and education in this country, a we will do everything in our po

to *step up* pressure on the Government and force them to *back down*. We must *speak out against* this policy and make it clear that it is unacceptable.'

A member of the Cabinet, speaking on behalf of the Government, ruled out any change in policy.

'The Government is not going to *climb down over* this issue. There will be no U-turns. We have made the right decision and we are gr. *stick to it*.'

H outcome of .e is by no means 'eral Government ising to back their y. Some political

commentators are predicting the downfall of the Government or a politically embarrassing climb-down. What is certain is that if the Opposition win the vote, it will be a serious setback for the Prime Minister and could *bring down* the Government. There has been mounting criticism of the Government's performance recently, and now the Prime Minister himself is coming under fire from members of his own party. Last night he tried to *play down* the seriousness of the situation. When asked about the crisis, he replied: 'Crisis? What crisis? There is no crisis.'

Checking understanding

Match the multi-word verbs in A with the definitions in B.

A	B
1 to call for something	a. to increase or intensify the speed, degree, quantity or quality of something
2 to stand up for someone/ something	b. to continue to support something, not abandon or change something
3 to stand for something	c. to defend someone/something that is under attack
4 to step something up	d. to express your views forcefully and publicly
5 to back down/climb down (over something)	e. to represent certain ideas or attitudes
6 to speak out (against something)	f. to make something appear less important than it really is
7 to stick to something	g. to demand something
8 to bring someone/something down	h. to cause someone/something to lose power or be defeated
9 to play something down	i. to admit you are wrong in an argument or dispute and agree to do what someone wants you to do

Drills

T.8

Listen to the sentences on the tape. Use the prompts you hear to make sentences with the same meaning.

Example
We are demanding a change in the law. (call for)
We are calling for a change in the law.

53

Practice

1 Work in pairs. Read the newspaper extracts below. Then re~~ing~~ the multi-word verbs from the boxes.

| call for | bring down | stand for | back down | step up |

Yesterday, the Opposition claimed it is the only party that represents social justice and the needs of ordinary people. They have increased pressure on the Government recently by demanding a general election this summer. They believe they will defeat the Government unless it admits it is wrong over its new economic policy.

| climb down over | play down | speak out against | stick to |

Despite pressure from the Opposition, the Government has announced it will not withdraw its new economic policy. They say they will continue with the policy because it is the right one. Several political commentators believe the Government is trying to make the crisis appear less serious than it really is. If the economic situation does not improve soon, some Government MPs may begin to criticize their own party openly.

Collocation

2 Which of the words can be used with the multi-word verbs below? Up to three items may be correct.

1 We want to bring down
   a. this corrupt regime.
   b. this football team.
   c. this new law.
   d. this building project.

2 We will step up
   a. security.
   b. our election campaign.
   c. taxes.
   d. expenditure.

3 The wrong multi-word verbs have been used in the political speech below. Correct them.

Our political party *speaks out against* equality and justice. We will never be afraid to *stand up for* corruption and inequality. We will always *play down* the weakest members of society. We want the government to *stick to* its policy of cutting expenditure on health and education. The government has tried to *step up* the present crisis by saying the situation isn't very serious, but we know what the truth is. That is why we are *climbing down over* an immediate general election.

4   Some nouns and adjectives come from multi-word verbs. Look at how the following are used in the text on page 52. Discuss with your partner what you think they mean.

a. a strong public *outcry*
b. he was particularly *outspoken* in his criticism
c. the *outcome* of Wednesday's vote
d. the *downfall* of the Government
e. a politically embarrassing *climb-down*
f. a serious *setback* for the Prime Minister

Now use the words above to complete the following sentences:

1 She's a very ____ critic of the government. She's not afraid to say what she thinks.
2 What do you think will be the ____ of the general election?
3 There was a general ____ when the government announced its intention to reduce pensions.
4 Nobody was sorry to see the ____ of the dictator.
5 Although the Minister said he would not abandon his policy, he was finally forced into a humiliating ____.
6 The poor results in the local elections have been a serious ____ for the government.

Idiomatic expressions

5   What do you think the following expressions mean?

1 to be up in arms (over/about something)
2 to make a U-turn (in something)
3 to come under fire

Think of examples for the following:

a. Situations in which people are up in arms about something.
b. Situations in which someone makes a U-turn.
c. Someone who has come under fire recently.

Role-play

6 Work in pairs. One of you is a TV interviewer, the other is a spokesperson for the Opposition. Read the notes for your role below, and spend some time thinking about what you will say, and how you can use the multi-word verbs and expressions from this unit. Then act the interview out.

TV Interviewer

The Government says it intends to cut public expenditure on health and education. During the interview try to find out the following:

- ❏ what the Opposition party represents
- ❏ why the Opposition is so angry about the Government's policy
- ❏ how the Opposition will increase pressure on the Government
- ❏ who will win next Wednesday's vote

Make the following points about the Government's position:

- ❏ the Government says it will not change its policy
- ❏ the Government says the situation is not serious and there is no crisis

---

Spokesperson for the Opposition

The Government says it intends to cut public expenditure on health and education. During the interview, make the following points:

- ❏ your party represents justice, equality, better health and better education
- ❏ you are going to increase pressure on the Government
- ❏ you are demanding a national debate on education and health
- ❏ you want the Government to change its policy
- ❏ the situation is more serious than the Government says it is
- ❏ MPs are criticizing the PM
- ❏ your ultimate aim is to defeat the Government

How multi-word verbs work

7 *down*

The particle *down* can be used with some verbs to give the idea of either defeat or suppression.
The scandal eventually brought down the government. (defeat)
The government is trying to hold down inflation. (suppression)

Look at the following sentences and say if the idea of either defeat or suppression is being expressed, or if it is a mixture of both.

a. The proposal was *voted down* at the meeting.
b. The management has *climbed down* in its negotiations with the unions.
c. The police are going to *crack down* on drug pushers.
d. The army was called in to *put down* the rebellion.
e. She tried to make her opinion known but she was *shouted down*.

What's the answer?

What is the difference between *to stand for something* and *to stand up for someone/something*?

Joke

A certain Prime Minister, who had a reputation for looking down on the members of the Cabinet, decided to take all of them out for a meal in a restaurant. The Prime Minister began by ordering fish.
'And the vegetables?' asked the waiter.
'Oh, they'll have fish too,' replied the Prime Minister.

Speaking

The Party Manifesto below was produced by the Government before the last general election. You think the Government has broken all its election promises. Discuss with your partner what you will say in a letter of complaint to your MP.

PARTY MANIFESTO

Our party represents social justice and good economic management.

Vote for us and if we are elected we will:

- *increase public expenditure*
- *fight for the old and sick people in our society*
- *publicly condemn any examples of corruption*
- *increase security against terrorist attacks*
- *always tell you the truth about any situation – no matter how bad it is*
- **NOT** *raise taxes*
- **NOT** *change our policies*

VOTE FOR US
THE PARTY YOU CAN TRUST

Writing

Write the letter of complaint to your MP. Remember to use the multi-word verbs and expressions you have learnt in this unit.

9 Happily ever after

Preparation

Work in pairs. Discuss the following questions.
- What makes some relationships between couples break up?
- What qualities do you think are needed for a lasting relationship?

Presentation

T.9a

Listen to two people, Helen and then George, talking about their marriages. Then discuss with your partner the questions below.

1 How did they meet their partners?
2 What did they think of their partners when they first met them?
3 What did their parents think of their partners?
4 How did Helen and George feel about marrying their partners?
5 Why did their marriages succeed or fail?

Checking understanding

Match the multi-word verbs in A with the definitions in B. If necessary, listen to the cassette again or look at Tapescript 9a on page 82.

A	B
1 to fall for someone	a. to compensate for something
2 to take to someone/something	b. to become friends again after an argument
3 to stand by someone	c. to provide help or support for someone when they are in trouble
4 to let someone down	d. to fall in love with someone
5 to look on someone as something	e. to consider someone as something
6 to see in someone/something	f. to find a particular quality in someone/something
7 to make up/to make it up (with someone)	g. to disappoint someone, often by breaking a promise or agreement
8 to grow apart (from someone)	h. to end a relationship or marriage
9 to make up for something	i. to begin to like someone/something
10 to split up	j. to develop separate interests and become gradually less close to someone

Drills

T.9b

Listen to the sentences on the tape. Use the prompts you hear to make sentences with the same meaning.

Example
I consider you to be someone I can trust. (*look on as*)
I look on you as someone I can trust.

Practice

1 In the conversations below, write the statements or questions for A that produced the responses for B.

Example
A *Do you think the two of you will ever split up?*
B No, I think we'll stay together for the rest of our lives.

1 A _____
  B Thank you for saying that. I consider you to be my best friend as well.

2 A _____
  B Yes, she really helped me when I was in trouble.

3 A _____
  B Good, I'm glad to hear the two of you are friends again.

4 A _____
  B Well, you could start by saying sorry.

5 A _____
  B No, after forty years we're still very close to one another.

6 A _____
  B Yes, I know. It's always a mistake to rely on him.

7 A _____
  B Have they? That's really surprising. I thought they were such a happy couple.

8 A _____
  B Yes, I was really surprised. I thought she wouldn't like skiing at all.

9 A _____
  B I hope you're right, because I think I've fallen in love with him.

10 A _____
  B I agree. I don't understand why she thinks he is special or interesting.

2 Work in pairs. Take turns to ask and answer the questions below. Try to use the multi-word verbs from the box.

look on someone as something		fall for someone
make it up	stand by someone	let someone down
grow apart	make up for something	split up

1 What is your idea of a good friend?
2 Who do you consider to be your best friend and why?
3 When was the last time someone disappointed you? What happened?
4 If you disappointed someone, how would you try to compensate for it?
5 What do you think are the most common reasons for people separating?

How multi-word verbs work

There are four basic types of multi-word verbs:

Type 1: intransitive and inseparable
Type 2: transitive and separable
Type 3: transitive and inseparable
Type 4: transitive and two inseparable particles

3 Look at the 10 multi-word verbs in italics in Tapescript 9a on page 82. How many of them can you categorize according to the four types? Which ones do not fit these patterns? Remember that some multi-word verbs can be more than one type.

Idiomatic expressions

4 Work with your partner. Discuss what you think the following expressions in italics mean.

1 It was *a turning-point* in my life.
2 He proposed to me completely *out of the blue.*
3 Life is full of *ups and downs.*
4 I started *to have second thoughts* about it.
5 I started to see her *in a different light.*
6 There has to be *give and take* in a relationship.

Now discuss the following points with your partner:

– examples of when you might need some give and take in a relationship
– why relationships have their ups and downs
– an important decision that you had second thoughts about
– something that has been a turning-point in your life
– someone or something that has made you see things in a different light

5 Work with your partner. Match expressions 1–6 to the pictures below. Then discuss how you would express the same ideas in your own language.

1 Love is blind
2 to be over the moon
3 to see the world through rose coloured spectacles
4 to have your head in the clouds
5 to be on cloud nine
6 to have your feet (firmly) on the ground

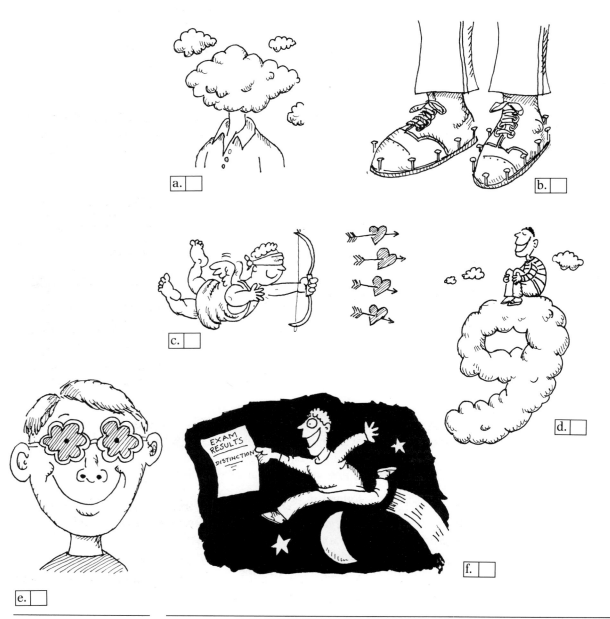

What's the answer?   What is the difference between

1 *to fall for someone* and *to take to someone?*
2 *to make up for something* and *to make up?*

Jokes

> **'What are you complaining about? You married me for better or for worse, didn't you?'**
> **'Yes, but the worse is much worse than I expected.'**

> **'What do you have in common with your husband?'**
> **'We got married on the same day.'**

Speaking   Work in pairs. Each study one problem situation below. Then take turns to describe the problem situation to your partner, and discuss the advice you would give. Try to use the multi-word verbs and expressions from this unit.

> **Student A**   Problem situation
> *You have a young sister who sees the world in a very naive and idealistic way. Last week she met a young man on a blind date and immediately fell in love with him. She says he is the ideal man for her, but you cannot understand what she finds wonderful or attractive about him. Your parents do not like him. Yesterday he unexpectedly asked her to marry him and she accepted. She is extremely happy but you think she is too young and naive.*
> *What should she do?*

> **Student B**   Problem situation
> *A friend of yours, Tom, has a very difficult relationship with his girlfriend. One moment their relationship is very good, and the next it is very bad. They often have arguments because neither of them will compromise about anything. Although in the end they are always friends again, you think the problem is that recently they have become less close to one another. Tom has told you he met someone else last week, and liked this person very much. He now feels differently about his girlfriend, and is thinking of ending their relationship. But he knows his girlfriend depends on him for help and support, and doesn't want to disappoint her.*
> *What should he do?*

When you have finished, report back to the rest of the class. Say if you agreed or disagreed with the advice that was given.

Writing   Either:
A friend has written to you with one of the problems above. Write a letter of reply, giving advice and using the multi-word verbs and expressions in this unit.

Or:
Write a story called 'The Blind Date'. Try to use the multi-word verbs and idiomatic expressions you have learnt in this unit.

10 It takes all sorts

Preparation

Work in pairs. Discuss the questions below.
- What do you understand by the expression *It takes all sorts to make a world?*
- Describe someone you consider to be strange or eccentric.

Presentation

T.10a

Listen to descriptions of three people. Make notes on what is strange about them. Then compare your notes with your partner.

1 _____

_____

2 _____

_____

3 _____

_____

Checking understanding

Match the multi-word verbs in A with the definitions in B. If necessary, listen to the tape again, or look at Tapescript 10a on page 83.

A	B
1 to be getting on for something	a. to begin to do something as a regular habit
2 to take to doing something	b. to be noticeable, conspicuous
3 to liven (something) up	c. to defend oneself against the attacks or demands of someone more powerful
4 to go on about somone/something	d. to try to impress people by making one's abilities very obvious, usually from pride or vanity
5 to pick on someone	e. to select someone repeatedly for criticism, punishment or blame
6 to stand up to someone	f. to be nearly a certain age or time, to be growing old
7 to show off	g. to make something more interesting, exciting and lively
8 to stand out	h. to stop participating in a course of study, a competition or society
9 to drop out (of something)	i. to keep talking about the same thing, usually to an annoying extent

Drills

T.10b

Listen to the sentences on the tape. Use the prompts you hear to make sentences with the same meaning.

Example
He didn't complete medical school. *(drop out)*
He dropped out of medical school.

Practice

1 Complete the sentences, using multi-word verbs from this unit.

a. The party was very dull so we tried to ____ by getting everyone to dance.
b. He started a three-year drama course, but he ____ after two months and found a job in a hotel.
c. I don't like him because he is so vain. He's always ____ in front of other people.
d. He decided to ____ his boss and refuse to accept his demands.
e. Although my grandmother ____ eighty, she still goes for a three-mile walk every morning before breakfast.
f. She believed the boss was ____ her because he never criticized anyone else in the office.
g. Her way of dressing made her ____ in a crowd.
h. He never used to touch alcohol, but recently he has ____ drinking in the pub all night.
i. She kept ____ her operation. It was very boring because we had heard it all before.

2 One of the sentences below is correct. All the others have one mistake in them. Change the sentences so that they are all correct.

a. She tried to live up the discussion by saying something controversial.
b. If he's always picking on you, you should stand up for him.
c. She gets on for ninety.
d. He makes himself stand up in a crowd by showing off.
e. He shouldn't have made the mistake of dropping out of college.
f. They're always going about the state of the economy.
g. She's taken to play golf at the weekends.

3 Work in pairs. Discuss the statements and questions below. Use the multi-word verbs from this unit.

a. How old is your oldest relative?
b. What would you do if someone was always selecting you for criticism or punishment?
c. How would you make a party more interesting and lively?
d. Have you ever felt you didn't want to complete a particular course? If so, why? What happened?
e. Think of someone who is always trying to draw attention to themselves in an obvious way. What do you think of this person?
f. Think of someone who is always talking about something in an annoying way.
g. Have you adopted any new habits recently? If yes, what are they?

Idiomatic expressions

4 1 Read your own star sign description, and those of other people you know. Discuss with your partner if they are accurate or not.
2 Try to guess which star signs belong to other people in your class.

Aquarius (JANUARY 20 – FEBRUARY 18)
You are practical and realistic about what is important in life – you have your feet firmly on the ground. You are intelligent and love thinking up new ideas but you sometimes *have a memory like a sieve*. Once you have made a promise, you never go back on it. You like change, and often wear outrageous clothes that make you stand out in a crowd.

Pisces (FEBRUARY 19 – MARCH 20)
You are sensitive, imaginative and creative, but also very emotional – your heart rules your head. You are not ambitious or materialistic and often have your head in the clouds. You are indecisive because you don't always *know your own mind*, but you are good at *putting yourself in other people's shoes*.

Aries (MARCH 21 – APRIL 20)
You are a born leader and like to dominate people. You are very active and rather impulsive, so you tend to do things *on the spur of the moment*. You lose your temper very easily, but you get over it quickly and can be quite charming. You're not good at following other people's advice, but you're quick to give advice to them.

Taurus (APRIL 21 – MAY 20)
You are practical, reliable, and determined. You have a *mind of your own* so it is very difficult to make you do something you don't want to. This means you can be stubborn at times. You like the security that comes from routine so you don't like change. You are loyal and generous to your friends and will stand by them whenever possible.

Gemini (MAY 21 – JUNE 20)
You are intelligent, interested in everything, and have an excellent general knowledge. You think and talk fast and you are full of restless energy. You are versatile and good at doing several things at the same time. You have a strong sense of humour and often *have your friends in stitches*. You are sociable, get bored easily and love change.

Cancer (JUNE 21 – JULY 21)
You are very sensitive and easily hurt. If someone says an unkind word to you, you *take it to heart*, but you are also very forgiving. Your family life is very important to you. You are sincere in love, but often take things too seriously. You are a loyal friend and have a good memory, but you can be moody sometimes.

Leo (JULY 22 – AUGUST 21)
You have a confident and attractive personality, but you tend to be proud. You like to *be in the public eye* and you are easily flattered. You love the sun and are very generous – indeed, you *have a heart of gold*. You like to organize other people, and you are quick to stand up for someone who you think is being attacked.

Virgo (AUGUST 22 – SEPTEMBER 21)
You are quiet and shy and don't like crowds. You tend to be a loner and *keep yourself to yourself*. You are a perfectionist – you want everybody and everything to be perfect and this makes it difficult for people to live up to your high standards. You prefer to play a supporting role at work and in relationships.

Libra (SEPTEMBER 22 – OCTOBER 22)
You are sympathetic, tolerant and a good listener, so when a friend needs *a shoulder to cry on*, they turn to you. Love is important for you and you are always falling for people. However, you are indecisive. You spend a long time weighing up all the possibilities before you make up your mind.

Scorpio (OCTOBER 23 – NOVEMBER 21)
You have strong likes and dislikes and tend to *see things in black and white*. As a result, you tend to make instant judgements and rarely change your mind about things or people. You are ambitious, but love is more important to you than success. You are very secretive and hide your true feelings. If you are hurt you always take revenge.

Sagittarius (NOVEMBER 22 – DECEMBER 20)
You are friendly, extrovert, and outspoken. You rebel against authority and have a tendency to *speak your mind* when it would be better to remain silent. You hate pretence and deception. You are intelligent and like to show off your knowledge to other people. You love travel and danger and you have a hot temper.

Capricorn (DECEMBER 21 – JANUARY 19)
You are a strong-minded person who takes life and work very seriously. Your talent and determination make you successful and you usually *get to the top*. In your relationships you are faithful and loyal, but you are also possessive and like to be in control. You are very cautious and tend to bottle up your feelings rather than release them.

5 Look at the horoscopes again. Discuss with your partner the meaning of the idiomatic expressions in italics.

6 Work with your partner. Discuss the points below.

1 Name three people who are often *in the public eye*.
2 Name three people who have *got to the top* in their profession.
3 Name someone who is not afraid to *speak their mind*.
4 When was the last time someone *had you in stitches*?
5 What have you done *on the spur of the moment* recently?
6 Do you have a *shoulder to cry on* when you are upset? If yes, who is it?

How multi-word verbs work

7 *into*
What is the general meaning of the particle *into* in the examples below?

1 When she heard the news she *burst into* tears.
2 One moment he was calm and reasonable, and the next moment he *flew into* a rage and started shouting at everyone.
3 He used to be a charming man but in later life he *turned into* a very unpleasant person.
4 She *settled into* the routine of her new job very quickly.
5 He *got into* the habit of watching TV every afternoon.

What's the answer?

What are the two different meanings of *to take to* in these sentences?

a. I *took to* him immediately.
b. I *took to* playing golf every Saturday morning.

Jokes

My cross-eyed teacher at school had to give up teaching.
Why?
Because he couldn't control his pupils.

Dear Sir,
I understand that next Monday's flight to Rome is fully booked, but I would like to have a seat with a good view if anyone drops out.

Writing

Write a description of someone who you think is strange or eccentric. Give details of their appearance, character, habits, and opinions. Try to use the multi-word verbs and expressions you have learnt in this unit.

Proverbs

Preparation

Work in pairs.
Discuss what you think the three proverbs below mean.

When in Rome, do as the Romans do

Birds of a feather flock together

All that glitters is not gold

What other English proverbs do you know? Explain what they mean.

Reading

Read the text and then answer the questions which follow.

Proverbs are popular short sayings of a moral or practical nature. To qualify as proverbs, the sayings must be old and contain some kind of enduring wisdom. They are used to give a word of advice or warning, or to make a wise general comment on a particular situation.

Obviously some proverbs are easier to understand than others. Those which say directly what they mean in straightforward language present the fewest problems.

The more you have, the more you want.

It's easy to be wise after the event.

In these examples there is no need to look for a truth beyond the literal sense of the words, because the proverb is itself a generalized truth. With other proverbs, however, it is necessary to transfer the specific meaning to a more general situation before it can be fully appreciated.

A stitch in time saves nine.

Here the proverb refers to mending clothes. If you mend a small tear with a few stitches immediately, you avoid the necessity of mending a large tear later on. In other words, prompt action at an early stage can prevent more serious trouble developing in the future.

As for the origin of proverbs, they probably date back to the time when wisdom was transmitted by story or song. Some can be traced back to early Greek and Latin sources, but it is difficult to say with any certainty where others originated, because they were often translated from language to language.

Shakespeare is the greatest literary source of sayings and proverbs in English, though no one is certain how many of them were the product of his own thought, and how many were part of the oral tradition of his time.

Neither a borrower nor a lender be.

All that glitters is not gold.

These, and the sayings and proverbs of other major authors of the past, have entered the language and become part of the culture because of their universal appeal or truth.

A thing of beauty is a joy forever.   (John Keats)

A little learning is a dangerous thing.   (Alexander Pope)

However, some proverbs are much more widely used than others. Indeed, the acceptance and rejection of proverbs throughout the ages can be seen as a history of the changes that have occurred in the manners, morals, and social development of a country. For example, the proverb *A stitch in time saves nine* is not used very frequently now, and sounds rather old-fashioned because few people spend their time mending clothes in today's throwaway society – they just go out and buy new ones. But even if people do not use proverbs very much in their daily lives, almost everybody knows them. Some are so well-known that it is only necessary to say the first part of the proverb – the rest will be understood immediately.

When in Rome ... (do as the Romans do)

Birds of a feather ... (flock together)

If your first language is not English and you try to use proverbs, you run the risk of sounding rather artificial and unnatural, especially if you over-use them or produce them in inappropriate contexts. You also have to be word perfect when you use them, because they are fixed expressions. Perhaps the most natural way to introduce them into a conversation is to say

Well, you know what they say ...

You may decide not to use them actively, but it is certainly worth learning them for recognition purposes, and they can provide you with an insight into the culture of the country. In the words of the philosopher and scientist Francis Bacon

'The Genius, Wit and Spirit of a Nation are discovered in its Proverbs.'

1 Why are some proverbs more difficult to understand than others?
2 Why is it sometimes difficult to find the origin of a proverb?
3 Why are some proverbs more often used than others?
4 What advice is given about proverbs?

Presentation and Practice

1a.

1b.

Sort the following words into well-known proverbs. The first word has been given in each case.

a. crying   milk   it's   use   over   no   spilt

It's _____

b. is   life   the   spice   variety   of

Variety _____

c. eat   cake   it   can't   you   have   and   your

You _____

d. the   pudding   proof   the   of   the   eating   in   is

The _____

How would you express the same ideas in your own language?

1c.

1d.

2 Match the two halves of the proverbs below. The first one has been done for you.

1 When in Rome,
2 If you want a thing done properly,
3 It takes all sorts
4 Where there's a will,

5 All work and no play
6 If at first you don't succeed,
7 Laugh and the world laughs with you,
8 Two's company,
9 When the cat's away,

a. three's a crowd.
b. try, try, try again.
c. there's a way.
d. weep and you weep alone.
e. makes Jack a dull boy.
f. do it yourself.
g. do as the Romans do.
h. the mice will play.
i. to make a world.

3 Some sayings are so well-known that it is only necessary to say the first part of the sentence.

Example
– Are you coming to the party on Friday night?
– No, I want to revise for my exams.
– Well, you know what they say, 'All work and no play...'

Work with your partner. Make similar short dialogues in which you use only the first part of the sayings from exercise 2.

English proverbs and their international equivalents
The meaning of some proverbs is common to many different cultures.
Some of these can be translated literally from one language to another,
but with some proverbs the same meaning is expressed in different ways.

4 Match the English proverbs below with their international equivalents.
(F = French; G = German; I = Italian; S = Spanish; T = Turkish)

English proverbs
1 You can't have your cake and eat it.
2 A leopard never changes its spots.
3 Don't cross your bridges before you come to them.
4 Give him an inch and he'll take a mile.
5 You're making a mountain out of a molehill.
6 Don't count your chickens before they're hatched.
7 Don't put the cart before the horse.
8 A bird in the hand is worth two in the bush.
9 It's the last straw that breaks the camel's back.
10 You scratch my back and I'll scratch yours.

International equivalents
a. Don't put the bridle on the tail of the horse. (G)
b. One hand washes the other. (G)
c. You can't have your barrel full of wine and your wife drunk. (I)
d. A wolf loses its hair but not its vices. (I, G)
e. Don't roll up your trousers before you see the river. (T)
f. Don't sell the bearskin before you have caught it. (F)
g. You're making an elephant out of a fly. (G)
h. Better an egg today than a hen tomorrow. (I)
i. Give him your little finger and he'll take your hand. (G)
j. It's the last drop that makes the glass overflow. (S)

Can you think of other examples?

5 Some proverbs have the same meaning, while others seem to contradict one another. Look at the examples below and group them into pairs of proverbs which have the same meaning and pairs of proverbs which contradict one another.

1 Moderation in all things.
2 He who hesitates is lost.
3 Out of sight, out of mind.
4 Enough is as good as a feast.
5 There's no arguing about tastes.
6 Look before you leap.
7 Absence makes the heart grow fonder.
8 Many hands make light work.
9 One man's meat is another man's poison.
10 Too many cooks spoil the broth.

Similar meaning: Opposite meaning:

_____   _____

_____   _____

_____   _____

_____   _____

Listening

T.11

Listen to the situations on the tape. Give an appropriate proverb for each of them.

Joke

> During a performance at a theatre, there was a power cut and all the lights suddenly went out. A man on stage stepped forward and apologized. Then he asked everyone in the audience to put their hands up in the air. They did so – and to their great surprise, the lights came back on.
> 'How did you do that?' someone asked.
> 'Very simple,' he replied. 'Many hands make light work.'

Speaking

1 Work with your partner. Think of a dialogue which illustrates one of the proverbs in this unit. Act it out without saying the proverb. The rest of the class must provide the appropriate proverb.

2 Which of the proverbs in this unit will you remember? Why?

Writing

Write a story that illustrates, or ends with, a proverb from this unit.

Tapescript section

Unit 1

Tapescript 1a

D: Doctor   **N:** Nurse

D Good morning, nurse. How are things on the ward today?

N Very quiet at the moment, doctor.

D How's Mr Harris getting on?

N He's fine. He had his operation early this morning and he's still under the anaesthetic at the moment, but it seems he's *come through* it very well.

D Good. I think he'll need at least a week to *build up* his strength, but after that he should be up and about pretty quickly. How's Mr Stephens?

N The surgeons decided to *go ahead with* the operation last night, and at first we were rather worried – we thought he wasn't going to *come through* it, but he seems to be over the worst now and his condition is stable.

D Well, he's in good hands, and I'm sure you'll do an excellent job of looking after him. I think we may need to give him some antibiotics to *fight off* any possible infection. And Mr Spencer?

N I'm afraid he took a turn for the worse in the night. He died early this morning.

D I see. Have his relatives been informed?

N Yes, they have.

D What about Mr King? Has there been any change?

N There's been an improvement in his condition, but he's in pain when the effect of the drugs he's taking starts to *wear off*, and he says he's had some attacks of breathlessness.

D Has he told you what *brings* them *on*?

N No, but I know he hasn't given up smoking. Old habits die hard, I suppose... At the moment he says he doesn't *feel up to doing* anything – he just wants to lie in bed and rest. Should he keep on taking the tablets?

D Yes, for the moment – it's best to be on the safe side. But we'd like to *try out* a new course of treatment *on* him. I think I'll go and have a word with him now...

Tapescript 1b

Listen to the sentences. Then say the sentences again, using the multi-word verb prompts. The first one has been done for you.

1 Would you like to test this new product?
   (*try out*)
   Would you like to try out this new product?
2 She survived a very serious illness.
   (*come through*)
   She came through a very serious illness.
3 I'm trying to get rid of a cold at the moment.
   (*fight off*)
   I'm trying to fight off a cold at the moment.
4 The pain is beginning to disappear.
   (*wear off*)
   The pain is beginning to wear off.
5 They've decided to proceed with the treatment.
   (*go ahead with*)
   They've decided to go ahead with the treatment.
6 Reading in a poor light can cause headaches.
   (*bring on*)
   Reading in a poor light can bring on headaches.
7 I'm too tired to see anybody today.
   (*feel up to*)
   I don't feel up to seeing anybody today.
8 You must strengthen your muscles.
   (*build up*)
   You must build up your muscles.

Unit 2

Tapescript 2

Listen to the sentences. Then say the sentences again, using the multi-word verb prompts. The first one has been done for you.

1 The government has introduced new drinking laws.
(*bring in*)
The government has brought in new drinking laws.

2 The government hasn't kept its election promises.
(*go back on*)
The government has gone back on its election promises.

3 The whole matter will soon be forgotten.
(*blow over*)
The whole matter will soon blow over.

4 The government tried to hide the truth.
(*cover up*)
The government tried to cover up the truth.

5 She proposed a solution to the problem.
(*put forward*)
She put forward a solution to the problem.

6 The police are being stricter with drivers who break the speed limit.
(*crack down on*)
The police are cracking down on drivers who break the speed limit.

7 Following allegations of corruption, the chairman decided to resign.
(*stand down*)
Following allegations of corruption, the chairman stood down.

8 This candidate hasn't got the right qualities for the job.
(*be up to*)
This candidate isn't up to the job.

9 The Prime Minister said we must all accept our responsibilities.
(*face up to*)
The Prime Minister said we must all face up to our responsibilities.

10 He persuaded many people to support him.
(*win over*)
He won many people over.

Unit 3

Tapescript 3a

P: Presenter   **J:** Julia

P Hello, and welcome to *Arts Review*. In today's programme we'll be talking about Sheila Gold's latest novel, *One Hot Summer*, the new production of *The Tempest* at the National Theatre, and the new John Allen film. Here to discuss them with me is Julia Webb.

J Hello.

P First, the writer Sheila Gold. She's just *brought out* her latest novel, *One Hot Summer*. It's about a young girl who goes to spend the summer with her uncle and later discovers his true identity. What did you *make of* it, Julia?

J I thought it was quite an enjoyable book in places, but the storyline was very complicated, so it wasn't a complete success.

P Yes, it took me a long time to work out precisely what was *going on*. What did you *make of* the ending?

J I thought the so-called 'surprise' ending didn't work – it just didn't *come off*. The fact that her uncle *turns out* to be her real father wasn't a surprise at all.

P So this wasn't a story that made you want to go and read more of her novels.

J No, I'm afraid it wasn't. In fact, it *put me off* reading any more of her work.

P So let's move on to Joanne Passman's new production of *The Tempest*. It's had excellent write-ups in the press. What were your impressions? Did it *live up to* your expectations?

J Yes, it certainly did. I was expecting something special, but this was more than that – it was superb! I thought the sense of mystery and magic *came across* very powerfully.

P I agree completely. I think it's by far her best production and I'm sure it will be a huge success.

J Yes, it's definitely a production not to be missed.

P And finally, let's talk about John Allen's new film, *Suburban Blues*.

J Mm ... I found it amusing at times, but dark and melancholy at others, so it wasn't at all clear what message he was trying to *put across*.

P Yes, it's had very mixed reviews.

J I thought the music and the photography were out of this world, but as for the storyline, well, I couldn't make head or tail of it. And the hero's behaviour at the end was completely out of character.

P Yes, I had mixed feelings about it, too. And there, I'm afraid, we'll have to leave you till next week.

Tapescript 3b

Listen to the sentences. Then say the sentences again, using the multi-word verb prompts. The first one has been done for you.

1 I didn't understand what was happening.
(*go on*)
I didn't understand what was going on.
2 She's very good at conveying her ideas.
(*put across*)
She's very good at putting across her ideas.
3 The plan for saving the company was excellent, but it didn't succeed.
(*come off*)
The plan for saving the company was excellent, but it didn't come off.
4 They're going to publish a new edition of her poems.
(*bring out*)
They're going to bring out a new edition of her poems.
5 The reviews discouraged me from reading the book.
(*put off*)
The reviews put me off reading the book.
6 The play wasn't as good as I thought it would be.
(*live up to*)
The play didn't live up to my expectations.
7 The message of the play was understood very clearly.
(*come across*)
The message of the play came across very clearly.
8 What was your impression of him?
(*make of*)
What did you make of him?
9 In the end they discovered he was the murderer.
(*turn out*)
In the end he turned out to be the murderer. OR
In the end it turned out that he was the murderer.

Unit 4

Tapescript 4

Listen to the sentences. Then say the sentences again, using the multi-word verb prompts. The first one has been done for you.

1 I was completely deceived by his charming manner.
(*take in*)
I was completely taken in by his charming manner.

2 I never base my judgements on first impressions.
(*go by*)
I never go by first impressions.
3 She could see what kind of man he was immediately.
(*see through*)
She saw through him immediately.
4 She pretended to be an American tourist.
(*pass off*)
She passed herself off as an American tourist.
5 She gave the impression of being a very kind person.
(*come across as*)
She came across as (being) a very kind person.
6 He persuaded me to lend him some money.
(*talk into*)
He talked me into lending him some money.
7 You won't escape being punished for this!
(*get away with*)
You won't get away with this!
8 The police told him to give them the gun.
(*hand over*)
The police told him to hand over the gun.

Unit 5

Tapescript 5a

1 A self-made woman

I come from a very poor background. My parents never had any money so we literally lived from hand to mouth. That's probably why I *set out* to become rich before I was thirty. I found a job in a company, and when I'd saved up enough money I started up my own business. What do I *put* my success *down to*? Hard work. You have to work hard for what you want in this life.

2 A rich woman

I'm fortunate because I *came into* a lot of money when my aunt died and left me everything. I invested the money and now I *live off* the interest. I suppose I'm what you would call well-off – but money isn't everything. Sometimes it creates more problems than it solves.

3 A bankrupt businessman

At one time I was extremely well-off, but then came the stock market crash and I lost everything. I had no money to *pay off* my debts and I was declared bankrupt. What did I learn from this experience? Firstly, money doesn't grow on trees, and secondly, when you lose everything you find out who your real friends are – they're the ones who stay with you when you come down in the world.

4 Unemployed person

The last job I had was so badly paid that I couldn't make ends meet on my salary, and as a result I was always getting into debt. Everything was becoming more expensive all the time but my salary stayed the same, so I couldn't *keep up with* the cost of living. My bank account was in the red and I had no savings to *fall back on*. And then I lost my job. Now things are really hard and I have to *get by on* less than £50 a week. I know they say money can't buy happiness, but I'd rather be rich and unhappy than poor and unhappy.

5 A middle-aged regular saver

Some people spend money like water, but not me – I believe in saving up for a rainy day. I *put by* a little money every week. You see, you have to think about the future when you're my age. When you're young you don't need money but when you're old, you can't live without it.

Tapescript 5b

Listen to the sentences. Then say the sentences again, using the multi-word verb prompts. The first one has been done for you.

1 I've repaid all my debts.
 (*pay off*)
 I've paid off my debts.
2 I save a little money every week.
 (*put by*)
 I put by a little money every week.
3 He inherited a fortune when his father died.
 (*come into*)
 He came into a fortune when his father died.
4 She survives on a very small income.
 (*get by on*)
 She gets by on a very small income.
5 She gets all her money from her parents.
 (*live off*)
 She lives off her parents.
6 My salary isn't rising as fast as inflation.
 (*keep up with*)
 My salary isn't keeping up with inflation.
7 We thought her bad behaviour was the result of stress.
 (*put something down to*)
 We put her bad behaviour down to stress.
8 I know I can always ask my parents for help if I'm ever in trouble.
 (*fall back on*)

I know I can always fall back on my parents if I'm ever in trouble.
9 She intended to become the best tennis player in the world.
 (*set out to*)
 She set out to become the best tennis player in the world.

Unit 6

Tapescript 6

Listen to the sentences. Then say the sentences again, using the multi-word verb prompts. The first one has been done for you.

1 The police prevented anyone entering or leaving the area.
 (*seal off*)
 The police sealed off the area.
2 She established an organization to help young offenders.
 (*set up*)
 She set up an organization to help young offenders.
3 He confessed to stealing the money.
 (*own up to*)
 He owned up to stealing the money.
4 His boss only gave him a warning.
 (*let off*)
 His boss let him off with a warning.
5 He let the police arrest him.
 (*give oneself up*)
 He gave himself up to the police.
6 They want to conduct a medical examination.
 (*carry out*)
 They want to carry out a medical examination.
7 The bomb exploded at four in the afternoon.
 (*go off*)
 The bomb went off at four in the afternoon.
8 After two years of peace, war suddenly began.
 (*break out*)
 After two years of peace, war broke out.
9 Negotiations between management and unions have collapsed.
 (*break down*)
 Negotiations between management and unions have broken down.
10 I was surprised by her change in attitude.
 (*take aback*)
 I was taken aback by her change in attitude.

Unit 7

Tapescript 7a

P: Presenter   **S:** Sally (radio reporter)
J: Joanne (a company director)

P In today's programme, we'll be looking at how companies are doing during these difficult times of recession. Our reporter, Sally Green, went to talk to Joanne Wade, director of a soft drinks company.

S So, Joanne, can you tell me how your individual products are doing?

J Well, we brought out *Bubble Up* over a year ago and initially it got off to a bad start, but after an intensive advertising campaign the idea of the drink *caught on* and then sales *picked up* very quickly. It's now our most successful product and is selling like hot cakes.

S I understand you're planning to bring out a new drink called *Fizzy Cola*.

J Yes, that's right. It should be on the market next summer, though we're a little behind schedule at the moment. We were going to build the advertising campaign around a famous pop star, but unfortunately that *fell through*. So we had to abandon the whole idea and start from scratch.

S What will the new approach be?

J We've *come up with* the idea of using a successful athlete instead. That way we should attract people who like sports.

S And how is the company itself doing in these difficult times of recession?

J Well, last year our annual turnover was £25million and we *took on* extra staff, but this year sales have *fallen off*, so we've had to *lay off* a hundred workers. We've also decided to *back out of* an expensive project to produce a new kind of chocolate drink.

S A lot of companies have gone to the wall because of the downturn in the economy. Do you think your company is in any danger?

J No, I don't. Things are difficult for everyone at the moment, but we're managing to keep our heads above water. In fact, if things improve a little we may *take over* another company.

S And what about the future?

J We're hoping for an upturn in the economy. If this happens, then sales might start to *pick up*, but no one can be certain. At the moment it's a question of wait and see.

Tapescript 7b

Listen to the sentences. Then say the sentences again using the multi-word verb prompts. The first one has been done for you.

1 We employ extra staff at Christmas.
   (*take on*)
   We take on extra staff at Christmas.
2 She produced several excellent ideas.
   (*come up with*)
   She came up with several excellent ideas.
3 He gained control of the company.
   (*take over*)
   He took over the company.
4 The economy is improving.
   (*pick up*)
   The economy is picking up.
5 The demand for our product is decreasing.
   (*fall off*)
   The demand for our product is falling off.
6 The government has withdrawn from the project.
   (*back out of*)
   The government has backed out of the project.
7 The company has temporarily dismissed three hundred workers.
   (*lay off*)
   The company has laid off three hundred workers.
8 The plan to build another airport was abandoned.
   (*fall through*)
   The plan to build another airport fell through.
9 Her ideas have become really popular.
   (*catch on*)
   Her ideas have really caught on.

Unit 8

Tapescript 8

Listen to the sentences. Then say the sentences again, using the multi-word verb prompts. The first one has been done for you.

1 The Opposition has increased its attacks on the government.
   (*step up*)
   The Opposition has stepped up its attacks on the government.
2 The aim of the rebels is to defeat the government.
   (*bring down*)
   The aim of the rebels is to bring down the government.

3 The Opposition Party is demanding a general election.
   (*call for*)
   The Opposition Party is calling for a general election.
4 We must defend our democratic rights!
   (*stand up for*)
   We must stand up for our democratic rights!
5 What does your political party represent?
   (*stand for*)
   What does your political party stand for?
6 We must express our views forcefully against the war.
   (*speak out*)
   We must speak out against the war.
7 We will not abandon our policy.
   (*stick to*)
   We will stick to our policy.
8 The government is reducing the importance of the latest unemployment figures.
   (*play down*)
   The government is playing down the latest unemployment figures.
9 The government has admitted it was wrong.
   (*back down OR climb down*)
   The government has backed down. OR
   The government has climbed down.

Unit 9

Tapescript 9a

I: Interviewer   **H:** Helen

I How did you meet your husband?
H It was on a blind date, actually. A friend invited me to meet someone she knew. She said he was very nice, so I went along, and as soon as I met him, I *fell for* him. I thought he was wonderful. We started to go out with one another, and then I invited him home to meet my parents, and they *took to* him immediately – they thought he was a lovely person.
I So meeting him was an important event?
H Oh, yes, it was a turning-point in my life. You see, whereas I'd always had my head in the clouds, he was very practical and realistic – he had his feet firmly on the ground.
I Do you remember when he asked you to marry him?
H Yes, very clearly. We were walking in the park and he proposed to me completely out of the blue. I really wasn't expecting it.
I How did you feel about marrying him?

H I was over the moon. I thought it was the most wonderful thing that could ever have happened to me.
I And do you still feel that way today?
H Oh, yes, we're devoted to one another.
I What do you think has made your marriage such a success?
H The fact that we've always supported and helped one another. I've always *stood by* him, and he's never *let me down* once. We're a partnership.
I So you never have any arguments?
H Well, we have our ups and downs now and then – everybody does – but I know that underneath it all we were made for each other.

I: Interviewer   **G:** George

I How did you meet your wife?
G We worked for the same company. She was about the same age as me, and she struck me as a very nice person. As time passed I came to *look on* her as a friend. We spent some time together and then we started going out with one another.
I What did your parents think of her?
G When I introduced her to my mother she said she couldn't understand what I *saw in* her. She thought she was very ordinary and not at all the right person for me.
I Do you think your mother's opinion influenced you in any way?
G I think it made me have second thoughts about marrying her, but we still got married a few months later.
I What was life like after you got married?
G Things were all right for a while but then we began to quarrel. We always kissed and *made up* in the end, but there were still problems between us.
I Why was that?
G I think the main thing was that we weren't really suited to one another. After we got married we started to see one another in a different light. We spent less and less time together, we became interested in different things, and gradually we *grew apart*.
I What happened then?
G We started having terrible arguments and I behaved very badly towards her. I tried to *make up for* it, but she couldn't forgive me. In the end we *split up*. I suppose it was inevitable really.
I And how did this experience affect you?
G I think it changed my outlook on life. I certainly don't see it through rose-coloured spectacles any more.

I Would you marry again?

G I would, but it would have to be the right person, and there would have to be a lot more give and take. Otherwise I don't think it would work.

Tapescript 9b

Listen to the sentences. Then say the sentences again, using the multi-word verb prompts. The first one has been done for you.

1 When I was in trouble she gave me help and support.
(*stand by*)
When I was in trouble she stood by me.

2 I have always considered you to be my closest friend.
(*look on as*)
I have always looked on you as my closest friend.

3 I'm depending on you, so don't disappoint me!
(*let down*)
I'm depending on you, so don't let me down!

4 The children liked her the moment they met her.
(*take to*)
The children took to her the moment they met her.

5 She fell in love with her skiing instructor.
(*fall for*)
She fell for her skiing instructor.

6 I don't understand what she finds attractive about him.
(*see in*)
I don't understand what she sees in him.

7 She tried to compensate for the trouble she had caused.
(*make up for*)
She tried to make up for the trouble she had caused.

8 After a year they ended their relationship.
(*split up*)
After a year they split up.

9 I think we've become less close to one another.
(*grow apart*)
I think we've grown apart.

10 They had an argument but later they became friends again.
(*make up*)
They had an argument but later they made up. OR
They had an argument but later they made it up.

Unit 10

Tapescript 10a

1 Aunt

My aunt's *getting on* for sixty, and she's always been a very dynamic sort of person, but recently she's started to behave in a rather strange way. A few months ago she took up karate and judo, and now she's *taken to* riding a powerful motorbike everywhere she goes. Last week she turned up at my sister's birthday party dressed in a leather jacket with *Hell's Angels* written on the back. 'I've come to *liven things up*,' she said, and immediately began dancing wildly to loud rock music. My sister found it rather embarrassing.

'I wish she'd act her age,' she said. 'She behaves as if she were sixteen rather than sixty.' But it doesn't bother me at all. It takes all sorts to make a world.

2 Art Teacher

I remember my art teacher because she was always *going on about* Van Gogh's paintings. In fact, they were the only thing she ever talked about and in the end we got rather tired of hearing about them. And for some strange reason we were never allowed to use yellow in our pictures. If we did, she'd stamp her feet and shout: 'That's yellow! I won't have yellow in my class!'

But the main reason I remember her is that she used to *pick on* my best friend at school. She always chose her to punish or humiliate in front of the other pupils. On one occasion she said, 'Look at this girl's work. It's the worst in the class!' And then she suddenly started laughing. My poor friend put up with this for a whole year, and then one day she decided to *stand up to* her. 'Stop *picking on* me!' she said. 'And if I want to use yellow in my pictures, I will!' With that, my art teacher burst into tears and from that day on we could use any colours we liked.

3 Cousin

The strangest person I know is my cousin. He was an only child, and was used to being the centre of attention, so he tended to *show off* a lot in front of other people. I can't say he changed very much when he grew up. On his eighteenth birthday he shaved off all his hair and started wearing a safety-pin through his nose. I suppose he thought it would make him *stand out* in a crowd. He went to university but *dropped out* after only one week – he said he wanted to graduate from the university of life. The last thing I heard, he was trying to join a circus.

Tapescript 10b

Listen to the sentences. Then say the sentences again, using the multi-word verb prompts. The first one has been done for you.

1 She must be nearly ninety.
 (*get on for*)
 She must be getting on for ninety.
2 His strange clothes made him very noticeable.
 (*stand out*)
 His strange clothes made him stand out.
3 Why is the boss always criticizing me?
 (*pick on*)
 Why is the boss always picking on me?
4 She decided to confront her boss.
 (*stand up to*)
 She decided to stand up to her boss.
5 He tried to make the party more exciting and lively.
 (*liven up*)
 He tried to liven up the party.
6 She's always trying to impress people.
 (*show off*)
 She's always showing off.
7 He's always talking about his life in the army.
 (*go on about*)
 He's always going on about his life in the army.
8 He's started coming home late at night.
 (*take to*)
 He's taken to coming home late at night.
9 She withdrew from the course.
 (*drop out*)
 She dropped out of the course.

Unit 11

Tapescript 11

Listen to the situations on tape and give an appropriate proverb for each of them.

1 Your friend thinks that a piece of modern sculpture is beautiful. You think it is very ugly. You can't agree about it.
2 You take a job as a hotel receptionist and you meet some very strange people. At first you are rather surprised and shocked, but then you learn to accept it.
3 You are very angry because a friend has made a joke about you. Your friend thinks you're over-reacting.
4 Your friend accidentally breaks an expensive present and is very upset about it. You tell your friend not to be unhappy about something that cannot be changed.
5 You always go on holiday with your friend to the same place every year. Your friend is bored with this place and says it would be more interesting to visit many different places.
6 You see your friend in the park having a romantic conversation with someone. You decide it would be better not to start talking to your friend in these circumstances.
7 You make a mistake at work. All your colleagues tell you what you should have done. You think it is easy for them to say this after the result is known.
8 Your boyfriend or girlfriend is going abroad for several months. You are afraid that he or she will forget you while he or she is away.
9 You are having difficulties finding a job. You believe that if you are determined, you will eventually find one.
10 Your boss is very strict and will be away at a conference for two weeks. You think this will be a good opportunity to have some fun at work.

Answer key

Introductory unit

1 *to stand for something* = to be an abbreviation for
                      something
  to go off = to go bad, become sour or rotten (e.g. drink
      or food)
  to stand in for someone = to take the place of someone
                    who is absent

2 a. L
  b. N *to break something off* = to discontinue something,
                   to end something abruptly
  c. N *to drop off*   = to fall asleep
  d. L
  e. N *to stand up for someone/something*
                   = to defend someone/
                   something that is under
                   attack
  f. N *to turn something over in your mind*
                   = to consider something
                   carefully and at length
  g. L
  h. N *to fall through*   = to be abandoned or fail to
                   be completed (e.g. a plan or
                   arrangement)
  i. L
  j L

3 a. S
  b. N *to take off* = to leave the ground and begin flying
  c. S
  d. S
  e. N *to set off* = to begin a journey
  f. N *to make off* = to leave in a hurry, often in order
      to escape

With this group of verbs the particle *off* gives the idea of
departure or *movement away from somewhere.*

4 With this group of verbs the particle *off* gives the idea of
disconnection or *stopping something.*

5 1 e.   2 d.   3 f.   4 b.   5 a.   6 c.

6 Some meanings of *to go off*:
  1 This milk has *gone off*. (= to go bad, turn sour)
  2 The bomb *went off* without warning. (= to explode)
  3 The alarm clock *went off* at six o'clock. (= to make a
    sudden ringing noise)
  4 I liked him at first, but now I've *gone off* him. (= to
    stop liking someone)
  5 All the lights suddenly *went off*. (= to stop operating)
  6 The demonstration *went off* smoothly. (= to take
    place, happen)

Some meanings of *to blow up*:
  1 They *blew up* the bridge. (= to destroy something
    with explosives)
  2 The car *blew up*. (= to explode)
  3 She *blew up* the photograph. (= to enlarge)
  4 The affair has been *blown up* by the media. (= to
    exaggerate)
  5 He *blew up* his car tyres. (= to inflate)
  6 A storm is *blowing up*. (= to develop)

7 1 *to call something off* = to cancel an arrangement or
    special event.
    All the items here can be cancelled, but only a. and
    b. are correct.   c. Wrong. This is not a special event.
    d. Wrong

  2 *to break up* = to come to an end, involving people
    separating or leaving in different directions. All the
    items here can come to an end, but only a. and d.
    are correct.   b. Wrong. A film is not a group of
    people.   c. Wrong.

8 a. Type 4   b. Type 1   c. Type 2   d. Type 3
  e. Type 3   f. Type 1   g. Type 1   h. Type 4
  i. Type 2   j. Type 2

9 Type 1: *hit back, run out, get on, drop off, ring back*
Type 2: *hit someone back, put someone up, ring someone back*
Type 3: *look for something*
Type 4: *run out of something, stand up for someone, get on with something*

10 Some of these verbs have multiple meanings.

  a. *to bring someone up* = to raise a child
  to bring something up = to mention something or introduce it for discussion
  b. *to look something up* = to find information in a reference book
  to look someone up = to visit someone informally (informal).
  c. *to give up* = to admit defeat
  to give something up = to stop doing something
  d. *to make up* = to become friends again after an argument
  to make something up = to invent something (e.g. a story, an excuse)
  e. *to turn in* = to go to bed (informal)
  to turn someone in = to hand someone over to the police (informal)

Unit 1 In good hands

Presentation

Possible answers:

People: surgeon, anaesthetist, physiotherapist
Places: operating theatre, out-patient clinic, X-ray department
Treatment: surgeon, transplant, radiation, physiotherapy

Checking understanding

1 e.   2 d.   3 f.   4 g.   5 b.   6 c.   7 a.   8 h.

Practice

1 a. came through   b. fight off   c. feel up to
d. brought on   e. go ahead   f. wears off/wore off
g. try it out   h. build my strength up

Collocation

3 1 a. Wrong. You can only *fight off* something that is attacking or threatening you.   b. Correct
c. Wrong. You can't *fight off* pain by yourself – you need the help of drugs or medicine to do it.
d. Wrong

2 a. Correct   b. Correct   c. Wrong. Falling in love is something that happens naturally and does not require a sustained effort. If you don't *feel up to* doing something, then you don't have the necessary energy or desire to do something.   d. Wrong. Recovering from an illness is a natural process that does not require a sustained mental and physical effort.

3 a. Correct   b. Wrong.   You *go ahead with* a plan or an arrangement, or something for which permission has been requested.   c. Correct   d. Correct

4 a. Wrong. A cold is not a serious illness. But you can *get over* a cold or *fight off* a cold.   b. Wrong. An injury is not a serious illness or situation, but the result of an accident.   c. Correct   d. Correct

5 a. Wrong.   b. Wrong. Only feelings and sensations can *wear off*, e.g. enthusiasm, tiredness, pain, depression, strangeness, etc.   c. Correct   d. Correct

Idiomatic expressions

4 a. *to be up and about* = to recover from an illness and be in good health
b. *to be over the worst* = to start to improve after an illness
c. *to be in good hands* = to be looked after or cared for very well
d. *to take a turn for the worse/better* = to become suddenly worse/better during an illness
e. *Old habits die hard* = it is difficult to give up a habit you have had for a long time
f. *to be on the safe side* = to do something as a precaution in case something unexpected or unpleasant happens

How multi-word verbs work

5 a. *to live through something* = to experience and survive difficult times (e.g. war, famine)
b. *to go through something* = to experience, endure, or suffer something unpleasant (e.g. an operation, a lot of pain)
c. *to sit through something* = to remain seated until something, often unpleasant or boring, is completely finished (e.g. a meeting, a film)
d. *to sleep through something* = to remain completely asleep despite noise or disturbance
e. *to talk something through* = to discuss a problem or idea completely until an agreement is reached

The particle *through* can be used with some verbs to give the idea of completing something, e.g. to complete an experience (*live through, go through*), to complete a period of time (*sit through*, *sleep through*), or to complete a discussion (*talk through*).

6 Possible answers

a. The help of relatives and friends, religion, prayer.

b. You might leave because you are wasting time and sitting near the door, or you might stay because you paid for the ticket and you are not sitting near the aisle.

c. To get a different perspective, or because a problem shared is a problem halved.

What's the answer?

To *fight something off* is about defeating something, e.g. a cold or an infection. To *come through something* is about surviving something, e.g. an operation.

Unit 2 Floating voters

Preparation

floating voter = someone who is not a fixed supporter of any political party.

Checking understanding

1 c.   2 f.   3 h.   4 a.   5 e.   6 g.   7 i.   8 j.
9 d.   10 b.

Practice

1 a. A new law on smoking in public places has been brought in.

b. The government tried to cover up its involvement in the gun-running scandal.

c. It is rumoured that the Prime Minister will stand down before the next election.

d. Everybody is talking about the seriousness of the problem, but I think it will soon blow over.

e. The police are beginning to crack down on young criminals.

f. That's an excellent plan. Are you putting it forward to the Committee?

g. The government seems unable to face up to the problems created by its own policies.

h. The new man is well-qualified, but he isn't up to doing the job properly.

i. The new government promised not to raise taxes, but it went back on its promise.

j. Election campaigns are designed to win over more people to a particular party.

Collocation

2 1 a. Wrong. You *cover up* some kind of wrongdoing, such as a crime or error.   b. Correct   c. Correct   d. Correct

2 a. Wrong. You *crack down* on something that breaks a rule or law.   b. Wrong. Promotion is a good thing.   c. Correct   d. Correct

3 a. Correct   b. Wrong. A plan is an intention, not a promise or agreement.   c. Correct   d. Correct

4 a. Wrong. You *face up to* something that is hard and difficult to accept, such as a responsibility or task, so you have to face up to the *responsibility* of having children.   b. Correct   c. Correct   d. Correct

5 a. Correct   b. Correct   c. Correct   d. Wrong. You can only *bring in* a new law, rule or system.

6 a. Wrong. You *stand down* from a position of power or importance.   b. Wrong   c. Correct   d. Correct

7 a. Wrong. You *put forward* something such as a plan, scheme or solution so that it can be considered. b. Correct   c. Wrong   d. Correct

8 a. Correct   b. Correct   c. Wrong. You *are up to* a standard or task.   d. Correct

3 Possible responses:

a. Someone might want to *stand down* because they can't *face up to* their responsibilities, they *are not up to* the job, or because they tried to *cover up* something wrong but were discovered.

b. President Nixon tried to *cover up* his involvement in the Watergate scandal.

c. They try to *win people over* by saying they will *bring in* new laws and *crack down on* corruption, by *putting forward* popular policies, and by saying they will not *go back on* their election promises.

d. I think the police should *crack down on* drug pushers.

e. I would like the government to *bring in* more laws to protect the environment.

Idiomatic expressions

4 a. *to be out of step with something* = not to be in agreement, harmony or conformity with something

b. *to keep an open mind* = to avoid forming an opinion or making a decision about something until all the facts are known

c. *to turn a blind eye to something* = to pretend not to notice something that would normally be criticized or punished

d. *to be out of touch with something* = to have no recent knowledge or information about something

e. *to be/hang in the balance* = to be undecided, at a critical point

Expression c. has a negative connotation, expression b. has a positive connotation.

5 a. I want to keep an open mind.

b. His life hangs/is hanging in the balance.

c. I am out of touch with recent developments.

d. He turned a blind eye.

e. Her opinions on this matter are out of step with those of the majority of people.

How multi-verb words work

6 a. Type 2   b. Type 1   c. Type 2   d. Type 2
e. Type 2   f. Type 1

What's the answer?

1 to keep your word/promise

2 to be/keep in touch with something

3a. *to bring something in* = to introduce a law, rule or system, but *to put something forward* = to offer an idea or proposal

3b. The meaning is similar, but you can only *stand down* from a position of power or importance.

Unit 3 Arts review

Presentation

One Hot Summer
Positive points: quite enjoyable in places.
Negative points: storyline was complicated, so it took a long time to work out what was going on; surprise ending didn't work, it didn't *come off*; not a surprise when uncle *turns out* to be the real father; the book *put her off* reading any more of her work.

The Tempest
Positive points: had excellent write-ups in the press; it was superb; sense of mystery and magic *came across* very powerfully; Joanne Passman's best production by far; sure it will be a huge success.

Suburban Blues
Positive points: amusing at times; the music and photography were out of this world.
Negative points: dark and melancholy at times; not clear what message John Allen was trying to *put across*;

it's had mixed reviews in the press; storyline was impossible to understand – couldn't make head or tail of it; hero's behaviour at the end was out of character.

Checking understanding

1 g.   2 b.   3 i.   4 a.   5 h.   6 d.   7 c.   8 f.   9 e.

Practice

1 a. Susan Shaw brought out a slim volume of poetry last year.

b. Our attempt to climb the mountain in winter didn't come off.

c. Her behaviour was so strange that I didn't know what to make of her.

d. The author put across her ideas in very simple language.

e. I couldn't understand what was going on at the beginning of the film.

f. I thought the message of the play didn't come across very clearly.

g. The newspaper reviews put people off seeing the play.

h. I expected the music to be wonderful, but it didn't live up to my expectations.

i. At the end of the film it turns out that the hero is an American spy/the hero turns out to be an American spy.

2 a. Incorrect. *To come off* is used to talk about the success of a specific idea, plan or attempt.

b. Correct.

c. Correct.

d. Incorrect. *To come across* is used to talk about the communication of an idea or message, not about a whole book.

e. Incorrect. *To make of something* is usually used as a question (e.g. What do you make of it?) or in a negative statement (e.g. I didn't know what to make of it).

f. Incorrect. You don't form an impression of capital punishment.

g. Correct.

Idiomatic expressions

3 a. *out of this world* = fantastic, marvellous

b. *out of character* = something not typical of a person's usual behaviour

c. *to have mixed feelings about something* = to have both negative and positive feelings about something

d. *I can't make head or tail or it* (informal expression) = I can't understand it at all

How multi-word verbs work

5 a. The film had an excellent write-up in The Times.
   b. The show is a sell-out.
   c. The play is about the gradual break-up of their marriage.
   d. The film is about a prison break-out.
   e. She is trying to make a comeback.

What's the answer?

1 A writer or director *puts across* ideas, but the ideas *come across* to the reader or audience. *To put something across* is Type 2, separable and transitive. *To come across* is Type 1, intransitive and inseparable.

2 *To put something off* = to postpone something (Type 2), but *to put someone off doing something* = to discourage someone from doing something.

Unit 4 Going by appearances

Checking understanding

1 d.   2 b.   3 a.   4 e.   5 h.   6 c.   7 f.   8 g.

Practice

1 a. see through   b. passing himself off   c. had been taken in   d. go by   e. came across   f. talked me into   g. hand over   h. get away with

2 a. No, you can't have the money. I refuse to hand <u>it</u> over.
   b. She came across <u>as</u> a very decisive person.
   c. They got away <u>with</u> several serious crimes.
   d. He passed <u>himself off</u> as a policeman.
   e. You should have seen <u>through him</u> immediately.
   f. Correct
   g. He talked me into sig<u>nin</u>g the cheque.
   h. I never go <u>by</u> first impressions.

3 Possible answers:

1 No, I never *go by* first impressions because I think they are usually wrong.
2 I probably *come across* as rather shy.
3 I think you shouldn't go by appearances, otherwise you can be easily *taken in.*

4 My brother *talked me into* having a holiday with him and it was a disaster.

5 I would *pass myself off* as a famous film star so I could visit Hollywood.

Idiomatic expressions

4 a. *Once bitten, twice shy.* = if one is deceived or has an unpleasant experience, one is more careful the next time
   b. *Appearances can be deceptive.* = the way something looks does not always reflect its true nature
   c. *Honesty is the best policy.* = dishonesty may seem more profitable for a short time, but in the long run there are more advantages in being honest

How multi-word verbs work

5 1 She talked me into buying a new coat.
   2 The robbers tricked the bank manager into thinking they were genuine customers.
   3 The Mafia frightened him into remaining silent.
   4 She was forced into selling her house in order to pay off her debts.
   5 The government was shamed into taking action.

What's the answer?

to talk someone out of doing something

Unit 5 Money! Money! Money!

Checking understanding

1 f.   2 e.   3 d.   4 b.   5 i.   6 h.   7 g.   8 c.   9 a.

Language note: *to live off someone* can sometimes have a negative connotation, e.g. *He lives off his parents* suggests he is unreasonably dependent on them for his income.

Practice

1 a. Many pensioners have to get by on very little money.
   b. He calculated it would take him three years to pay off all his debts.
   c. She accumulated a great deal of money by putting by a little every week.
   d. His uncle died and he came into a fortune.
   e. She set out to start her own business.
   f. If I ever get into financial difficulties, I know I can always fall back on my brother for help.

g. She lives off the money she gets from selling her books.

h. She put her success down to luck.

i. My salary isn't keeping up with the cost of living.

2 Possible answers

a. ...I'd invest it and live off the interest.

b. ...to learn to play the piano well.

c. ...I'd look for another job.

d. ...I didn't have to support other people.

e. ...the increase in unemployment.

Idiomatic expressions

3 a. to live from hand to mouth

b. money doesn't grow on trees

c. to come/go down in the world

d. to make ends meet

e. to spend money like water

f. a rainy day

How multi-word verbs work

5 1 with   2 to   3 on   4 to   5 on   6 to   7 as
8 with   9 with   10 on

What's the answer?

a. to be in the black

b. to come/go up in the world

Unit 6 Crime doesn't pay

Preparation

Crime doesn't pay = crime does not provide you with any real profit because you are usually caught and punished in the end.

Checking understanding

1 i.   2 e.   3 b.   4 h.   5 g.   6 j.   7 c.   8 a.
9 f.   10 d.

Practice

1 1 A recent survey, *carried out* by a national newspaper, shows that the traditional two-parent family is *breaking down* and is gradually being replaced by single-parent families.

2 Bank robbers who managed to hide themselves in a time-lock safe in an attempt to steal £3 million, found they were unable to escape when their explosives failed to *go off*. They *gave themselves up* when security guards opened the safe two days later.

3 A woman whose 6-year-old daughter was killed by a drunk driver has complained that the judge *let the man off with* a six-month suspended sentence and a £250 fine. The Home Secretary has said he will be *setting up* a committee to look into the sentencing guidelines for such cases.

4 Shortly after the match, fighting suddenly *broke out* among the supporters of two rival football teams. The police *sealed off* the town centre in an attempt to contain the violence.

5 Jayne Wilson *owned up to* stealing £15,000 from the company where she worked, when she was caught red-handed by a security camera which recorded her placing the money in her briefcase. 'I was *taken aback* when I saw the recording,' said the managing director. 'I thought she was someone we could trust completely.'

Collocation

2 1 a. Correct   b. Correct   c. Wrong. This is the severest punishment possible. d. It depends on how serious the crime was. It is correct if the crime was very serious and the punishment is less than expected. It is wrong if the crime was not serious.

2 a. Correct   b. Wrong. You *set up* an organization or group of people to fulfil a task.   c. Correct
d. Correct

3 a. Correct b. Wrong. A committee is something you *set up* or establish.   c. Correct   d. Correct

4 a. Correct   b. Correct   c. Correct   d. Wrong. A telephone cannot *go off*, i.e. ignite or detonate.

5 a. Wrong. A film is not something that starts suddenly and violently, like a war or a fire.
b. Correct   c. Correct   d. Correct

6 a. Correct b. Wrong. This meaning of *to break down* is only used about the failure of relationships and communication between people.   c. Correct
d. Correct

3 Possible responses:

1 My alarm clock *goes off* at 6 a.m.

2 I would advise him to *give himself up to* the police and *own up to* the crime.

3 I would be *taken aback*. For example, if someone I
   thought was honest turned out to be a liar.
4 Injustice can cause riots to *break out*.
5 I would *let off* lightly the poor woman and the
   student.

Idiomatic expressions

4 a. *to catch someone red-handed* = to discover someone in
      the act of doing something wrong
   b. *to keep to the straight and narrow path/way* = to live in
      an honest way, in conformity to strict moral and
      religious principles, not getting involved with
      criminal or immoral activities (of Biblical origin)
   c. *poetic justice* = when someone is rewarded or
      punished in a perfectly suitable way, especially when
      it happens by chance
   d. *the punishment should fit the crime* = the punishment
      should be suitable for the crime, not too severe or too
      lenient
   e. *to take the law into your own hands* = to punish
      someone yourself according to your own ideas of
      justice, usually using force and breaking the law

How multi-word verbs work

6 The particle *off* is used with these verbs to give the idea
   of starting an explosive or violent reaction.
   a. *to let something off* = to cause something to explode
      (e.g. bomb, gun, cannon)
   b. *to spark something off* = to cause something violent to
      start (e.g. war, argument, debate, controversy, strike)
   c. *to go off* = to explode, detonate, or ignite, to make a
      sudden loud noise (e.g. bomb, alarm)
   d. *to trigger something off* = to cause something violent
      to start (e.g. war, fight, strike, debate, crisis)
   e. *to set something off* = to cause something to explode
      (e.g. fireworks, explosives)

What's the answer?

To set up an investigation is to establish or start an
investigation. *To carry out* an investigation is actually to
do the investigation itself.

Unit 7 Selling like hot cakes

Presentation

1 False. Initially it got off to a bad start. It was only
   after an intensive advertising campaign that the
   drink *caught on* and sales *picked up*.
2 True. The plan *fell through*. They had to start again
   from scratch.
3 False. Last year the company *took on* extra staff, but
   this year sales have *fallen off* and they have had to
   lay off a hundred workers. They also decided to *back
   out of* an expensive project to produce a new kind
   of chocolate drink.
4 False. The company is keeping its head above water
   and may *take over* another company.
5 False. If there is an upturn in the economy then sales
   might *pick up*, but no one can be certain.

Checking understanding

1 g.   2 d.   3 c.   4 h.   5 f.   6 e.   7 i.   8 a.
9 b.

Practice

1 are falling off   caught on   back out of   pick up
   take on   taking over   laying off   come up with
   fallen through

Collocation

2 1a. Correct   b. Wrong. You can only *come up with*
   something that is inventive, such as a suggestion, idea
   or solution.   c. Correct.   d. Correct
   2a. Correct.   b. Wrong. Only things which can become
   fashionable, such as a new idea, method, fashion, tune,
   or pastime, can *catch on*.   c. Correct.   d. Correct.
   3 a. Correct b. Wrong. Only something such as a plan
   or arrangement can *fall through*. But we can say 'the
   search has been abandoned/*called off*'.   c. Correct
   d. Correct
   4 a. Wrong   b. Wrong. Only things that can decrease
   in amount or number, such as sales, exports, economic
   growth, investment etc., can *fall off*.   c. Correct
   d. Correct

3 Possible answers:
   a. ...it was haunted.
   b. ...she wanted to run it more efficiently.

c. ...it was too expensive.
d. ...the colours were too bright.
e. ...they cut prices.
f. ...of a fall in demand.
g. ...of the poor pay and working conditions.
h. ...cleaning the atmosphere.
i. ...I could double their profits.

4 *turnover* = the value of the goods or services that a company sells during a particular period of time
downturn = a decrease in the level, rate or success of something
takeover = the act of taking control of a company by buying it or a majority of its shares
upturn = an improvement in something

a. downturn   b. takeover   c. turnover   d. upturn

Idiomatic expressions

5 a. to get off to a bad start
b. to sell like hot cakes
c. to start (something) from scratch
d. to go to the wall
e. to keep one's head above water

Possible answers:

1 I think a lot of companies will go to the wall.
2 The team got off to a bad start at the beginning of the season.
3 He decided to start again from scratch.
4 Our company is just managing to keep its head above water.
5 My friend's novel is selling like hot cakes.

How multi-word verbs work

7 a. The engine stopped working.
b. He stopped studying.
c. She stopped taking part in the competition.
d. The shop has stopped selling the jumpers because there aren't any more.
e. The species has stopped existing.
f. They have stopped being good friends.

What's the answer?

1 sales are picking up
2 to get off to a good/flying start
3 an upturn in the economy
4 to take someone on

Unit 8 Crisis? What crisis?

Presentation

1 There has been a strong public outcry; Opposition MPs were up in arms and *calling for* an emergency debate; they will do everything possible to make the Government *back down*; some Government MPs are refusing to back the Government.
2 They have ruled out any changes in policy; they are not going to *climb down*; there will be no U-turns; they will *stick to* their decision.
3 The outcome is by no means certain; the downfall of the Government is only a prediction; the Government can avoid defeat by *backing down*.
4 The PM is coming under fire from his own MPs; he is trying to *play down* the crisis.

Checking understanding

1 g.   2 c.   3 e.   4 a.   5 i.   6 d.   7 b.   8 h.
9 f.

Practice

1 Yesterday the Opposition claimed it is the only party that *stands for* social justice and the needs of ordinary people. They have *stepped up* pressure on the Government recently by *calling for* a general election this summer. They believe they will *bring down* the Government unless it *backs down over* its new economic policy.

Despite pressure from the Opposition, the Government has announced it will not *climb down over* its new economic policy. They say they will *stick to* the policy because it is the right one. Several political commentators believe the Government is trying to *play down* the crisis. If the economic situation does not improve soon, some Government MPs may begin to *speak out against* their own party.

Collocation

2 1 a. Correct   b. Wrong. You can only *bring down* something that is in a position of power, such as a government or dictator, not a football team, law, or project.   c. Wrong   d. Wrong
2 a. Correct   b. Correct   c. Wrong. You can *step up* things such as attacks and production, because you increase the quantity of something, and you can *step up* things like security, pressure, and a campaign because

these are things that you can intensify with extra effort and attention. But you cannot *step up* prices, taxes or expenditure because this is easily done and does not require extra effort.   d. Wrong

3 Our political party *stands for* equality and justice. We will never be afraid to *speak out against* corruption and inequality. We will always stand up for the weakest members of society. We want the government to *back/climb down over* its policy of cutting expenditure on health and education. The government has tried to *play down* the present crisis by saying the situation isn't very serious, but we know what the truth is. That is why we are *calling for* an immediate general election.

4 a. *an outcry* = an expression of strong disapproval or anger about something by the public or the media
b. *to be outspoken* = to express one's opinions or criticisms without worrying about the reaction or disapproval of other people
c. *an outcome* = the result of something
d. *the downfall of someone/something* = the ruin or failure of someone/something that is powerful
e. *a climb-down* = the act of admitting one is wrong and agreeing to accept the demands of someone else
f. *a setback* = an event that puts someone or something in a worse position than before.

1 outspoken   2 outcome   3 outcry   4 downfall
5 climb-down   6 setback

Idiomatic expressions

5 1 *to be up in arms (over/about something)* = to be very angry and protest about something because one is strongly opposed to it
2 *to make a U-turn (in something)* = to make a complete change in policy, direction, thinking, action, etc.
3 *to come under fire* = to be criticized strongly

How multi-word verbs work

7 a. defeat   b. defeat   c. suppression   d. defeat/ suppression   e. suppression

What's the answer?

to stand for something = to represent something, but *to stand up for someone/something* = to defend someone/ something that is under attack

Unit 9 Happily ever after

Presentation

Helen

1 She met her future husband on a blind date.
2 She *fell for* him immediately. She thought he was wonderful.
3 Her parents thought he was a lovely person and *took to* him immediately.
4 She was over the moon. She thought it was the most wonderful thing that could ever have happened to her.
5 They are devoted to one another. They have always supported and helped one another. She has always *stood by* him, and he's never *let her down*. They are made for each other.

George

1 He met his wife at work.
2 He thought she was very nice and he gradually came to *look on* her as a friend.
3 His mother couldn't understand what he *saw in* her, she thought she was very ordinary and not the right person for him.
4 He had second thoughts about it, but still got married a few months later.
5 They weren't really suited to one another. They saw one another in a different light after getting married. They *grew apart*, they had terrible arguments, he behaved badly and she couldn't forgive him. They *split up*.

Checking understanding

1 d.   2 i.   3 c.   4 g.   5 e.   6 f.   7 b.   8 j.
9 a.   10 h.

Practice

1 Possible answers:

1 I look on you as my best friend.
2 Did she stand by you?/She always stands by her friends.
3 We've made (it) up.
4 How can I make up for what I've done?
5 Have the two of you grown apart over the years?
6 He let me down again last night.
7 They've split up.
8 She really took to skiing.

9 I think he's fallen for you.

10 I don't understand what she sees in him.

2 Possible answers:

1 A good friend is someone who will *stand by* you in times of trouble, who will never *let you down*, and who will try to *make it up* with you if you have an argument.

2 I *look on* my sister as my best friend.

3 My brother *let me down*. He said he would take me with him to Paris but he didn't.

4 If I *let someone down*, I'd try to *make up for* it by doing something especially nice for them.

5 I think a lot of people *split up* because they *grow apart*, or they *fall for* someone else.

How multi-word verbs work

3 Type 1: grow apart, make up, split up

Type 2: let someone down

Type 3: fall for someone, take to someone/something, stand by someone, see in someone/something

Type 4: make up for something.

To look on someone as something is different.
To make it up and *to make it up with someone* are fixed expressions.

Idiomatic expressions

4 1 *a turning-point in something* = a moment when a very important change takes place

2 *out of the blue* = completely unexpected, without warning

3 *ups and downs* = a mixture of good and bad moments, happiness and sadness, success and failures, etc.

4 *to have second thoughts about something* = to have doubts about a decision one has made

5 *to see something in a different/new/fresh light* = to see something differently, e.g. as it appears in a particular situation

6 *give and take* = compromise, a willingness to do what someone else wants in order to reach a satisfactory result

5 1c. *Love is blind* = someone who is in love cannot see the faults of the loved one

2f. *to be over the moon* = to be very happy, delighted (informal)

3e. *to see the world through rose-coloured spectacles* = to see things as better or more pleasant than they actually are

4a. *to have your head in the clouds* = to be a dreamer, to be out of touch with reality, to have one's thoughts on other things

5d. *to be on cloud nine* = to be very happy (informal)

6b. *to have one's feet (firmly) on the ground* = to be practical and realistic

What's the answer?

1 *to fall for someone* = to have strong romantic feelings of love and attraction, but *to take to someone* = to begin to like someone

2 *to make up for something* = to compensate for something, but *to make up* = to become friends again

---

Unit 10 It takes all sorts

Preparation

It takes all sorts to make a world = the world is made of many sorts of people, and one should be tolerant of the differences

Presentation

1 Aunt: Although she's *getting on for* sixty, she recently took up karate and judo; has *taken to* riding a powerful motorbike; wears a leather jacket with *Hell's Angels* on the back; turned up at a party and danced wildly to rock music in order to *liven it up*; she doesn't act her age.

2 Art Teacher: She was always *going on about* Van Gogh's paintings; never allowed anyone to use the colour yellow; *picked on* speaker's best friend at school; burst into tears when a pupil *stood up to* her.

3 Cousin: He tends to show off; at eighteen shaved his hair off and started wearing a safety-pin through his nose; *dropped out of* university after one week in order to graduate from the university of life; wants to join a circus.

Checking understanding

1 f.   2 a.   3 g.   4 i.   5 e.   6 c.   7 d.   8 b.
9 h.

Practice

1 a. liven it up

b. dropped out

c. showing off

d. stand up to

e. is getting on for
f. picking on
g. stand out
h. taken to
i. going on about

2 a. She tried to live**n** up the discussion by saying something controversial.
  b. If he's always picking on you, you should stand up **to** him.
  c. She **is getting** on for ninety.
  d. He makes himself stand **out** in a crowd by showing off.
  e. Correct
  f. They're always going **on** about the state of the economy.
  g. She's taken to play**ing** golf at the weekends.

3 Possible responses:
  a. He/She is *getting on for* ...
  b. If someone was always *picking on* me I would *stand up to* them.
  c. I'd *liven it up* by dancing or playing loud rock music.
  d. I *dropped out of* studying Chinese because I found it too difficult.
  e. My cousin is always *showing off*.
  f. My brother is always *going on about* cars.
  g. I've *taken to* getting up earlier in the morning.

Idiomatic expressions

5 1 *to have a memory like a sieve* = to have a bad memory, forget things easily
  2 *to know one's own mind* = to know what one wants and have clear opinions
  3 *to put oneself in someone's shoes* = to imagine what it is like to be in someone else's position or situation
  4 *on the spur of the moment* = suddenly and without thinking
  5 *to have a mind of your own* = to have a strong and independent character, not be easily influenced by others
  6 *to have someone in stitches* = to make someone laugh uncontrollably
  7 *to take something to heart* = to be greatly affected or upset by something
  8 *to be in the public eye* = to be on TV and in the newspapers frequently, known by everyone
  9 *to have a heart of gold* = to be very kind and generous
  10 *to keep oneself to oneself* = to live quietly and not mix with other people

11 *a shoulder to cry on* = a person who listens to someone's problems and offers sympathy and understanding
12 *to see things in black and white (terms)* = to see things in a simple and uncomplicated way, not appreciating important details or complexities
13 *to speak one's mind* = to say clearly and openly what one thinks without fear
14 *to get to the top* = to achieve the greatest success, reach the most important position

How multi-word verbs work

7 The particle *into* can be used with some verbs to describe a process of change from one state to another.

What's the answer?

In sentence a., *to take to* = to begin to like someone/something.
In sentence b., *to take to* = to begin to do something as a habit or pastime.

Unit 11 Proverbs

Preparation

When in Rome do as the Romans do = when someone is away from home, they should adapt to the local customs
Birds of a feather flock together = people who have similar interests, tastes or character are often found together
All that glitters is not gold = do not judge something by its attractive appearance, as appearances can be deceptive

Reading

1 Some proverbs say what they mean in a simple and direct way, but with others you have to find a more general meaning from the literal meaning.
2 Because they were often translated from language to language.
3 Because of social development and the changes in manners and morals.
4 Do not overuse them, try to use them in appropriate contexts, and use them with complete accuracy.

Presentation and Practice

1 a. *It's no use crying over split milk* = there is no use being upset about something that cannot be changed, what's done cannot be undone

b. *Variety is the spice of life* = the chance to do different things and meet different people makes life more interesting and enjoyable

c. *You can't have your cake and eat it* = you have to choose between two things, you cannot have both

d. *The proof of the pudding is in the eating* = the only way to tell the real value of something is by putting it into practice or use

2 2 f.

3 i. *It takes all sorts to make a world* = the world is made of many sorts of people, and one should be tolerant of the differences

4 c. *Where there's a will there's a way* = if someone is determined to do something, they will find a way of doing it

5 e. *All work and no play makes Jack a dull boy* = someone who works all the time without any form of recreation becomes dull and uninteresting

6 b.

7 d.

8 a. *Two's company, three's a crowd* = if two people are happy together, it's better not to introduce the presence of a third person

9 h. *When the cat's away the mice will play* = when the person in authority is absent, the other people can do as they like and perhaps misbehave

4 1 c. 2 d. 3 e. 4 i. 5 g. 6 f. 7 a. 8 h.
9 j. 10 b.

A leopard never changes its spots = people cannot change their basic character or nature

Don't cross your bridges before you come to them = don't worry about things before they happen, as they may not happen

Give him an inch and he'll take a mile = if you agree to someone's demands in a small way, they will take advantage of you and want more

You're making a mountain out of a molehill = you're treating something as difficult or a serious problem when it is not

Don't count your chickens before they're hatched = don't be certain of success until it happens

Don't put the cart before the horse = don't do things in the wrong order

A bird in the hand is worth two in the bush = it is better to be content with what one has than to reject it in the hope of getting something better, as this may not happen

It's the last straw that breaks the camel's back = an additional small problem that makes an already difficult situation intolerable

You scratch my back and I'll scratch yours = if you help me or do me a favour, I'll help you

5 Similar meaning: 1 and 4, 5 and 9

1 *Moderation in all things* = one should avoid extremes

4 *Enough is as good as a feast* = enough is as good as a large quantity of something, so one should have reasonable needs

5 *There's no arguing about tastes* = everybody has different likes and dislikes, and taste is a personal thing, so it is a waste of time to argue about it

9 *One man's meat is another man's poison* = what is good or pleasing to one person may be bad or unsuitable for another

Contradictory meaning: 2 and 6, 3 and 7, 8 and 10

2 *He who hesitates is lost* = if someone does not make up their mind quickly, they can lose any chance of success

6 *Look before you leap* = consider something carefully before taking action

3 *Out of sight, out of mind* = someone or something that is not seen is soon forgotten

7 *Absence makes the heart grow fonder* = one feels more affection for someone when they are absent

8 *Many hands make light work* = the more people there are to do a task, the easier it is and the more quickly it is finished

10 *Too many cooks spoil the broth* = if too many people are involved in doing the same thing, it is spoilt because different people will want to do it differently.

Listening

Possible answers:

1 There's no arguing about tastes. OR
One man's meat is another man's poison.

2 It takes all sorts to make a world.

3 You're making a mountain out of a molehill.

4 It's no use crying over spilt milk.

5 Variety is the spice of life.

6 Two's company, three's a crowd.

7 It's easy to be wise after the event.

8 Out of sight, out of mind.

9 Where there's a will, there's a way. OR
If at first you don't succeed, try, try, try again.

10 While the cat's away, the mice will play.